HACKERS

KB132794

해커스 지텔프

수강료 최대 ▼

기출인강
200% 환급반

*[환급] : 목표 달성 시 / 교재비 환급대상 제외 / 제세공과금 본인부담

교재 최대 6권 + 응시료 반값 쿠폰 제공 ▼

해커스 지텔프
Jenna

해커스 지텔프
비비안

**지텔프 공식
기출문제 무료 제공**

*유의사항 참고

**핵심 출제 경향 반영
지텔프 적중특강 무료 제공**

*목표점수 미달성시 수강기간 +90일 무한 연장

**세무사 회계사 경영지도사 군무원
인강 115만원 상당 쿠폰제공**

| 세무사 환급반 할인 450,000원 | 군무원 인강 100,000원 |
| 회계사 환급반 할인 450,000원 | 경영지도사 환급반 할인 150,000원 |

*해당 패스 강의 한정 (유의사항 참고)

**그래머 게이트웨이
+보카어원편 인강 무료**

**해커스 지텔프
쉿!크릿플래너 제공**

*PDF

**학습지원
수강기간 100% 연장!**

최대 **90**일

*미션 실패시

상담 및 문의전화
해커스인강 02.537.5000

HackersIngang.com
지텔프 교재 받고 인강 무제한 수강하기 ▶

해커스 한국사능력검정시험 교재 시리즈

빈출 개념과 기출 분석으로 기초부터 문제 해결력까지
꽉 잡는 기본서

해커스 한국사능력검정시험
심화 [1·2·3급]

스토리와 마인드맵으로 개념잡고! 기출문제로 점수잡고!

해커스 한국사능력검정시험

2주 합격 **심화 [1·2·3급]** **기본 [4·5·6급]**

시대별/회차별 기출문제로 한 번에 합격 달성!

해커스 한국사능력검정시험

시대별/회차별 기출문제집 **심화 [1·2·3급]**

개념 정리부터 실전까지! 한권완성 기출문제집

해커스 한국사능력검정시험

한권완성 기출 500제 **기본 [4·5·6급]**

빈출 개념과 기출 선택지로 빠르게 합격 달성!

해커스 한국사능력검정시험

초단기 5일 합격 **심화 [1·2·3급]**
기선제압 막판 3일 합격 **심화 [1·2·3급]**

G-TELP KOREA 공식 지정

2주 만에 끝내는

해커스 지텔프 독해

LEVEL 2

해커스 어학연구소

최신 지텔프 출제 경향을 반영한
『해커스 지텔프 독해 Level 2』를 내면서

지텔프가 공무원, 경찰, 소방, 군무원 시험 등 점차 많은 곳에서 활용되면서, 많은 학습자들이 지텔프 공부에 소중한 시간과 노력을 투자하고 있습니다. 이에, 영어 교재 분야에서 항상 베스트셀러의 자리를 지키는 해커스의 독보적인 노하우를 담아, 지텔프 학습자들이 단기간에 목표 점수를 획득할 수 있는 효율적인 학습 방법을 제시하기 위해 『해커스 지텔프 독해 Level 2』 개정 2판을 출간하게 되었습니다.

지텔프 최신 출제 경향 반영!
지텔프 최신 출제 경향을 철저히 분석하여 교재 내 모든 내용과 문제에 반영하였습니다. 특히, 지텔프 독해 영역의 파트별 출제 패턴을 분석하여 해커스만의 학습 전략을 제시하였으며, 지텔프 최신 토픽 및 문제 출제 경향이 완벽 반영된 실전 문제들을 풍부하게 수록하여 지텔프 독해 영역에 완벽하게 대비할 수 있도록 하였습니다.

2주 만에 기본부터 실전까지 완성할 수 있는 기본서!
『해커스 지텔프 독해 Level 2』는 한 권으로 기본부터 실전까지 학습할 수 있는 구성입니다. 지텔프 독해 영역의 출제 패턴을 완벽하게 정리한 이론서이자 연습 문제부터 실전 문제까지 충분한 양의 문제를 수록한 실전서로, 기본을 다지려는 학습자부터 실전 감각을 높이고 목표 점수를 달성하려는 학습자까지 목적에 맞게 학습할 수 있습니다.

목표 점수 달성을 위한 다양한 학습자료!
학습자들이 교재를 더욱 효과적으로 활용할 수 있도록 해커스인강(HackersIngang.com)에서는 동영상강의와 지텔프 필수 단어암기장을 제공하며, 해커스영어(Hackers.co.kr)에서는 지텔프 학습 팁과 단기 고득점 비법 강의도 들을 수 있습니다.

『해커스 지텔프 독해 Level 2』가 여러분의 지텔프 목표 점수 달성에 확실한 해결책이 되고, 영어 실력 향상은 물론 여러분의 꿈을 향한 길에 믿음직한 동반자가 되기를 소망합니다.

해커스 어학연구소

CONTENTS

정답 · 해석 · 해설 [책 속의 책]

『해커스 지텔프 독해 Level 2』로
점수 잡는 비법

01. G-TELP 최신 출제 경향을 완벽하게 파악한다!

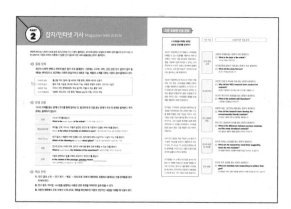

지텔프 최신 출제 경향을 철저히 분석하여 교재 내 모든 내용과 문제에 반영하였습니다. 지텔프 독해 영역에 출제되는 5가지 문제 유형부터 파트별 출제 패턴까지 상세히 설명하였으며, 최신 출제 경향을 완벽 반영한 문제들을 풍부하게 수록하여 독해 영역에 완벽하게 대비할 수 있도록 하였습니다.

02. 충분한 어휘 학습을 위한 학습 자료를 활용한다!

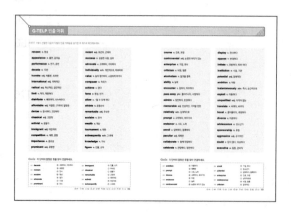

독해의 필수 요소인 어휘를 충분히 학습할 수 있도록 다양한 어휘 자료를 제공하고 있습니다. 문제 풀이에 필수적인 파트별 빈출 어휘뿐만 아니라, 매 시험마다 8문제씩 출제되는 어휘 문제의 정답률 100% 달성을 위한 기출 유의어 리스트까지 제공하여 목표 점수를 달성할 수 있도록 하였습니다.

03. 단계별 학습으로 기본부터 실전까지 완벽하게 대비한다!

| 문제 유형 공략하기 | → | PART별 출제 패턴 | → | HACKERS PRACTICE / TEST | → | 실전모의고사 |

문제 유형 공략하기에서 지텔프 독해 영역에 출제되는 5가지 문제 유형의 문제풀이 핵심 전략을 제시하였습니다. 또한, 파트별로 패턴화된 지문 흐름과 빈출 문제, 표현과 어휘를 학습할 수 있게 하였습니다. 그다음 HACKERS PRACTICE와 HACKERS TEST를 통해 실전 감각을 키울 수 있으며, 마지막으로 실전모의고사를 풀어봄으로써 시험에 보다 완벽하게 대비할 수 있도록 하였습니다. 해커스에서 제시하는 학습 플랜(p.20~21)을 통해 자신에게 맞는 학습 계획을 세우면 단기간에 기본부터 실전까지 완성할 수 있습니다.

04. 해커스만의 노하우가 담긴 학습자료를 200% 활용한다!

해커스인강(HackersIngang.com)에서 지텔프 필수 단어암기장과 단어암기 MP3를 무료로 이용할 수 있으며 본 교재의 유료 해설 강의를 수강할 수 있습니다. 또한, 온라인 토론과 정보 공유의 장인 해커스영어(Hackers.co.kr)에서 지텔프 학습 팁을 얻을 수 있으며 단기 고득점 강의를 수강할 수 있습니다.

G-TELP 소개

■ G-TELP란?

G-TELP란 General Tests of English Language Proficiency의 약자로 국제테스트 연구원(ITSC, International Testing Services Center)에서 주관하는 국제적 공인영어시험이며, 한국에서는 1986년에 지텔프 코리아가 설립되어 지텔프 시험을 운영 및 주관하고 있습니다. 듣기(Listening), 읽기(Reading), 말하기(Speaking), 쓰기(Writing) 평가 중심의 글로벌 영어평가 교육시스템으로, 현재 공무원, 군무원 등 각종 국가고시 영어대체시험, 기업체의 신입사원 및 인사·승진 평가시험, 대학교·대학원 졸업자격 영어대체시험 등으로 널리 활용되고 있습니다.

■ G-TELP의 종류

G-TELP에는 크게 G-TELP Level Test(GLT), G-TELP Speaking & Writing, G-TELP Jr., G-TELP B2B가 있습니다. 그 중에서 G-TELP Level Test(GLT)는 문법, 청취, 독해 및 어휘의 세 가지 영역의 종합 영어 능력을 평가하며, Level 1부터 5까지 다섯 가지 등급의 시험으로 구분됩니다. 한국에서는 G-TELP Level Test(GLT)의 다섯 Level 중 Level 2 정기시험 점수가 활용되고 있습니다. 그 외 레벨은 현재 수시시험 접수만 가능하며, 공인 영어 성적으로 거의 활용되지 않습니다.

구분	출제 방식 및 시간	평가 기준	합격자의 영어구사능력	응시자격
Level 1	청취 30문항(약 30분) 독해 및 어휘 60문항(70분) **총 90문항(약 100분)**	Native Speaker에 준하는 영어 실력: 상담, 토론 가능	외국인과 의사소통, 통역이 가능한 수준	Level 2 영역별 75점 이상 획득 시
Level 2	문법 26문항(20분) 청취 26문항(약 30분) 독해 및 어휘 28문항(40분) **총 80문항(약 90분)**	다양한 상황에서 대화 가능: 업무 상담 및 해외 연수 등 가능	일상 생활 및 업무 상담, 세미나, 해외 연수 등이 가능한 수준	제한 없음
Level 3	문법 22문항(20분) 청취 24문항(약 20분) 독해 및 어휘 24문항(40분) **총 70문항(약 80분)**	간단한 의사소통과 친숙한 상태에서의 단순 대화 가능	간단한 의사소통과 해외 여행, 단순 업무 출장이 가능한 수준	제한 없음
Level 4	문법 20문항(20분) 청취 20문항(약 15분) 독해 및 어휘 20문항(25분) **총 60문항(약 60분)**	기본적인 문장을 통해 최소한의 의사소통 가능	기본적인 어휘의 짧은 문장을 통한 최소한의 의사소통이 가능한 수준	제한 없음
Level 5	문법 16문항(15분) 청취 16문항(약 15분) 독해 및 어휘 18문항(25분) **총 50문항(약 55분)**	극히 초보적인 수준의 의사소통 가능	영어 초보자로 일상의 인사, 소개 등만 가능한 수준	제한 없음

■ G-TELP Level 2 구성

영역	내용	문항 수	배점	시간
문법	시제, 가정법, 조동사, 준동사, 연결어, 관계사	26개	100점	영역별 시험 시간 제한규정 폐지됨
청취	PART 1 개인적인 이야기나 경험담 PART 2 특정 주제에 대한 정보를 제공하는 공식적인 담화 PART 3 어떤 결정에 이르고자 하는 비공식적인 협상 등의 대화 PART 4 일반적인 어떤 일의 진행이나 과정에 대한 설명	7개 6개 6 or 7개 7 or 6개	100점	
독해 및 어휘	PART 1 과거 역사 속의 인물이나 현시대 인물의 일대기 PART 2 최근의 사회적이고 기술적인 묘사에 초점을 맞춘 기사 PART 3 전문적인 것이 아닌 일반적인 내용의 백과사전 PART 4 어떤 것을 설명하거나 설득하는 상업서신	7개 7개 7개 7개	100점	
		80문항	300점	약 90분

* 각 영역 100점 만점으로 총 300점이며, 세 개 영역의 평균값이 공인성적으로 활용되고 있습니다.

■ G-TELP 특장점

절대평가	빠른 성적 확인	3영역 객관식 4지선다형
상대평가가 아닌 절대평가이므로, 학습자가 공부한 만큼 목표 점수 달성 가능	응시일로부터 5일 이내의 빠른 성적 발표를 통해 단기간 영어 공인 점수 취득 가능	문법, 청취, 독해 및 어휘 3가지 영역의 4지선다형 객관식 문제로 보다 적은 학습 부담

G-TELP 시험 접수부터 성적 확인까지

1. 원서 접수

· **인터넷 접수:** 지텔프 홈페이지(www.g-telp.co.kr)에서 회원가입 후 접수할 수 있습니다.
· **방문 접수:** 접수기간 내에 지텔프 코리아 본사로 방문하여 접수할 수 있습니다.

2. 응시

· **응시일:** 매월 2~3회 일요일 오후 3시에 응시할 수 있습니다.
> * 정확한 날짜는 지텔프 홈페이지의 시험일정을 통해 확인할 수 있습니다.

· **입실 시간:** 오후 2시 20분까지 입실해야 하며, 오후 2시 50분 이후에는 절대 입실이 불가합니다.
· **준비물:**

| 신분증 | 컴퓨터용 사인펜 | 수정테이프 | 아날로그시계 | 단어암기장 |

- 수험표는 별도로 준비하지 않아도 됩니다.

- 시험 당일 신분증이 없으면 시험에 응시할 수 없으므로, 반드시 신분증(주민등록증, 운전면허증, 공무원증 등)을 지참해야 합니다. 지텔프에서 인정하는 신분증 종류는 지텔프 홈페이지(www.g-telp.co.kr)에서 확인 가능합니다.

- 컴퓨터용 사인펜으로 마킹해야 하며 연필은 사용할 수 없습니다. 연필이나 볼펜으로 먼저 마킹한 후 사인펜으로 마킹하면 OMR 판독에 오류가 날 수 있으니 주의합니다.

- 마킹 수정 시, 수정테이프를 사용해야 하며 수정액은 사용할 수 없습니다. 다른 수험자의 수정테이프를 빌려 사용할 수 없으며, 본인의 것만 사용이 가능합니다.

응시 관련 Tip

1. 고사장 가기 전
· 준비물을 잘 챙겼는지 확인합니다.
· 시험 장소를 미리 확인해 두고, 규정된 입실 시간에 늦지 않도록 유의합니다.

2. 고사장에서
· 1층 입구에 붙어 있는 고사실 배치표를 확인하여 자신이 배정된 고사실을 확인합니다.
· 고사실에는 각 응시자의 이름이 적힌 좌석표가 자리마다 놓여 있으므로, 자신에게 배정된 자리에 앉으면 됩니다.

3. 시험 보기 직전
· 시험 도중에는 화장실에 다녀올 수 없고, 만약 화장실에 가면 다시 입실할 수 없으므로 미리 다녀오는 것이 좋습니다.
· 시험 시작 전에 OMR 카드의 정보 기입란의 각 영역에 올바른 정보를 기입해둡니다.

4. 시험 시
· 답안을 따로 마킹할 시간이 없으므로 풀면서 바로 마킹하는 것이 좋습니다.
· 영역별 시험 시간 제한규정이 폐지되었으므로, 본인이 취약한 영역과 강한 영역에 적절히 시간을 배분하여 자유롭게 풀수 있습니다. 단, 청취 시간에는 다른 응시자에게 방해가 되지 않도록 주의해야 합니다.
· 시험지에 낙서를 하거나 다른 응시자들이 알아볼 수 있도록 큰 표시를 하는 것은 부정행위로 간주되므로 주의해야합니다. 수험자 본인만 인지할 수 있는 작은 표기만 인정됩니다.
· OMR 카드의 정답 마킹란이 90번까지 제공되지만, G-TELP Level 2의 문제는 80번까지만 있으므로 81~90번까지의마킹란은 공란으로 비워두면 됩니다.

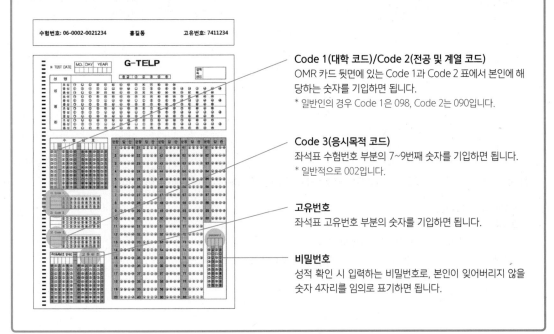

Code 1(대학 코드)/Code 2(전공 및 계열 코드)
OMR 카드 뒷면에 있는 Code 1과 Code 2 표에서 본인에 해당하는 숫자를 기입하면 됩니다.
* 일반인의 경우 Code 1은 098, Code 2는 090입니다.

Code 3(응시목적 코드)
좌석표 수험번호 부분의 7~9번째 숫자를 기입하면 됩니다.
* 일반적으로 002입니다.

고유번호
좌석표 고유번호 부분의 숫자를 기입하면 됩니다.

비밀번호
성적 확인 시 입력하는 비밀번호로, 본인이 잊어버리지 않을숫자 4자리를 임의로 표기하면 됩니다.

3. 성적 확인

성적표는 온라인으로 출력(1회 무료)하거나 우편으로 수령할 수 있으며, 수령 방법은 접수 시 선택할 수 있습니다. (성적 발표일도 시험 접수 시 확인 가능)

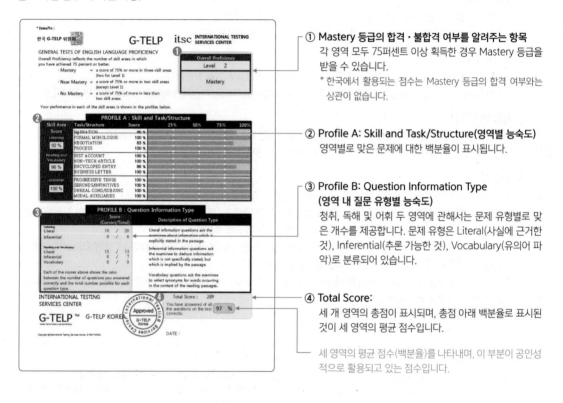

① **Mastery 등급의 합격 · 불합격 여부를 알려주는 항목**
각 영역 모두 75퍼센트 이상 획득한 경우 Mastery 등급을 받을 수 있습니다.
* 한국에서 활용되는 점수는 Mastery 등급의 합격 여부와는 상관이 없습니다.

② **Profile A: Skill and Task/Structure(영역별 능숙도)**
영역별로 맞은 문제에 대한 백분율이 표시됩니다.

③ **Profile B: Question Information Type**
(영역 내 질문 유형별 능숙도)
청취, 독해 및 어휘 두 영역에 관해서는 문제 유형별로 맞은 개수를 제공합니다. 문제 유형은 Literal(사실에 근거한 것), Inferential(추론 가능한 것), Vocabulary(유의어 파악)로 분류되어 있습니다.

④ **Total Score:**
세 개 영역의 총점이 표시되며, 총점 아래 백분율로 표시된 것이 세 영역의 평균 점수입니다.

세 영역의 평균 점수(백분율)를 나타내며, 이 부분이 공인성적으로 활용되고 있는 점수입니다.

🖩 G-TELP 학습 시 성적 계산법

점수는 아래의 공식으로 산출할 수 있습니다. 총점과 평균 점수의 경우, 소수점 이하 점수는 올림 처리합니다.

각 영역 점수: 맞은 개수 × 3.75
평균 점수: 각 영역 점수 합계 ÷ 3

예) 문법 20개, 청취 11개, 독해 및 어휘 23개 맞혔을 시,

문법 20 × 3.75 = 75점   **청취** 11 × 3.75 = 41.25점   **독해 및 어휘** 23 × 3.75 = 86.25점
→ **평균 점수** (75 + 41.25 + 86.25) ÷ 3 = 68점

★ G-TELP Level 2 성적 활용하기

정부 및 국가 자격증	기준 점수
국가공무원 5급	65점
외교관후보자	88점
국가공무원 7급	65점
국가공무원 7급 외무영사직렬	77점
입법고시	65점
법원행정고시	65점
소방공무원(소방장·소방교·소방사)	43점
소방간부 후보생	50점
군무원 5급	65점
군무원 7급	47점
군무원 9급	32점
카투사	73점
기상직 7급	65점
국가정보원	공인어학성적 제출 필수
변리사	77점
세무사	65점
공인노무사	65점
관광통역안내사	74점
호텔경영사	79점
호텔관리사	66점
호텔서비스사	39점
감정평가사	65점
공인회계사	65점
경찰공무원(경사·경장·순경)	43점
경찰간부 후보생	50점
보험계리사	65점
손해사정사	65점

* 그 외 공공기관 및 기업체에서도 지텔프 성적을 활용하고 있으며 지텔프 홈페이지에서 모든 활용처를 확인할 수 있습니다.

G-TELP 독해 소개 및 전략

1. 독해 출제 경향

① 4개 파트에서 한 지문씩 출제되며, 지문의 흐름이 패턴화되어 있습니다

PART 1 인물의 일대기 Biographical/Historical Article	· 특정 인물의 일대기를 시간 순서대로 서술하는 지문 · '인물 소개 → 유년 시절 → 주요 활동 → 근황 및 죽음'의 패턴화된 흐름
PART 2 잡지/인터넷 기사 Magazine/Web Article	· 사회적 이슈에 관한 기사 형태의 지문 · '연구 결과 소개 → 연구 계기 → 특징 → 의의/추후 과제'의 패턴화된 흐름
PART 3 지식 백과 Encyclopedia Article	· 인문학, 사회학, 과학 등 다양한 분야의 한 가지 소재를 소개하고 관련된 정보를 제공하는 백과사전식 지문 · '정의 → 기원 → 특징'의 패턴화된 흐름
PART 4 비즈니스 편지 Business Letter	· 서비스 홍보, 업무 요청 등을 하는 비즈니스 편지 지문 · '편지의 목적 → 요청 사항 및 답변 → 세부 설명 → 끝인사' 패턴화된 흐름

> 지텔프 독해 지문은 길고 내용이 많기 때문에, 이에 대비하기 위해서는 각 파트별 흐름을 익혀두는 것이 좋습니다.

> 한 지문은 보통 5~7개 단락으로 구성되어 있으며, 주로 각 단락에서 1문제씩 출제된다는 것을 알아두면 정답의 단서를 쉽게 찾을 수 있습니다.

② **5가지 문제 유형 중 특정세부사항 문제가 가장 많이 출제됩니다**

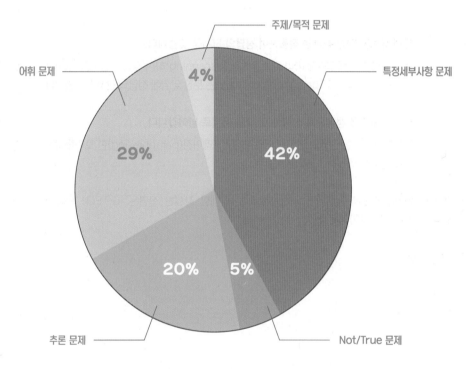

주제/목적 문제

어휘 문제

특정세부사항 문제

4%

29%

42%

20%

5%

추론 문제

Not/True 문제

▲ G-TELP 독해 문제 유형별 출제 비율

> 지문 전체를 다 읽을 필요 없이 문제가 묻는 내용을 담고 있는 부분의 한두 문장만 읽고 정답을 파악할 수 있는 특정세부사항 문제가 제일 많이 출제됩니다.

2. 문제 풀이 전략

다음 스텝에 따라 문제 풀이를 하면 빠르고 정확하게 문제를 풀 수 있습니다.

STEP 1 **각 문제를 먼저 읽고 문제 유형을 확인합니다.**

지문을 읽기 전에, 문제를 먼저 읽고 문제 유형이 무엇인지 확인합니다. 문제 유형은 질문의 형태로 구분할 수 있습니다.

STEP 2 **문제 유형별 핵심 전략을 적용하여 정답의 단서를 찾습니다.**

문제 유형별 핵심 전략에 따라 지문을 스캐닝(scanning)하여 정답의 단서를 찾습니다. 일반적으로 질문의 키워드가 패러프레이징(paraphrasing)되어 있는 문장 앞뒤에 정답의 단서가 있습니다.

STEP 3 **알맞은 보기를 정답으로 선택한 뒤 다음 문제로 넘어갑니다.**

지문에서 확인한 정답의 단서를 알맞게 패러프레이징(paraphrasing)한 보기를 정답으로 선택한 뒤, 다음 문제로 넘어가 STEP 1~3을 반복합니다.

* 스캐닝(scanning)과 패러프레이징(paraphrasing)에 대한 자세한 설명은 'G-TELP 독해 필수 스킬 Scanning & Paraphrasing'(p.18~19)에서 확인할 수 있습니다.

STUDY DEMONSTRATES MEN HAVE HIGHER RATE OF SEVERE CHRONIC DISEASE THAN WOMEN

A study in Harvard Men's Health Watch, a newsletter published by Harvard Medical School, demonstrated that the rate of severe chronic disease was higher among men than women. Furthermore, the article pointed out that men were more susceptible to die from the ten most common causes of death.

Citing data from the National Center for Health Statistics, the authors showed that stroke and Alzheimer's were the only maladies that affected women more or equal to men. Because of this disparity, male patients cost significantly more in health care than females despite being examined by physicians less.

(생략)

STEP 1

60번의 문제 유형을 확인합니다. 의문사 what을 사용하여 세부적인 내용을 묻고 있으므로 특정세부사항 문제임을 알 수 있습니다.

STEP 2

지문을 스캐닝하여 질문의 키워드 find out이 demonstrated로 paraphrasing된 것을 찾은 뒤 주변 내용을 주의 깊게 읽습니다.

60. What did the study find out?

   (a) that men tend to die younger than women

   (b) that health-care costs roughly similar regardless of gender

   (c) that men suffer from serious illness more than women

   (d) that women have stronger immune systems than men

STEP 3

지문의 단서 'the rate of severe chronic disease was higher among men than women'에서 남자가 여자보다 만성 질환을 앓을 확률이 높다고 했으므로, 이를 알맞게 표현한 (c)를 정답으로 선택한 뒤, 다음 문제로 넘어가 STEP을 반복합니다.

Scanning & Paraphrasing

지텔프 독해의 특징은 지문이 길더라도 문제는 아주 세부적으로 출제된다는 것입니다. 정답의 단서가 하나의 문장으로 되어 있는 경우가 많으므로, 지텔프 독해를 공략하기 위해서는 스캐닝과 패러프레이징을 먼저 익혀야 합니다.

1. Scanning (스캐닝) 세부사항 빠르게 찾기

스캐닝은 지문에 포함되어 있는 세부사항을 빠르게 찾아내기 위한 속독 방법입니다. 지텔프 독해에 출제되는 거의 모든 문제 는 질문의 키워드가 주어진 문장 혹은 그 앞뒤 문장의 내용만 파악해도 정답을 알 수 있습니다. 따라서, 스캐닝을 통해 문제 풀이에 필요하지 않은 정보는 빠르게 훑어보며 넘어가고 문제 풀이에 필요한 정보 위주로 자세하게 파악하여 문제를 푸는 것 이 중요합니다.

> **Scanning 적용방법**

(1) 문제가 묻는 것이 무엇인지 키워드를 정확히 파악합니다.

(2) 찾아야 하는 단서가 지문에서 어떤 형태로 등장할지 예상합니다.

　　예를 들어, 특정 사람에 관한 정보는 그 사람의 성, 이름뿐만 아니라 인칭대명사로도 등장할 수 있습니다.

(3) 지텔프의 패턴화된 지문의 흐름에서 찾아야 하는 단서의 위치를 예상합니다.

　　예를 들어, PART 1에서 인물이 유명한 이유는 인물을 소개하는 1단락에서 찾을 수 있습니다. 또한, 일반적으로 문제가 지 문 순서대로 나오기 때문에, 앞 문제의 정답 단서가 나온 다음 부분부터 스캐닝을 하는 것도 전략입니다.

2. Paraphrasing (패러프레이징) 바꾸어 표현하기

패러프레이징은 원래 문장에서 쓰인 표현을 다른 단어나 어구 또는 문장 구조 등으로 바꾸어 표현하는 것을 말합니다. 지텔프에 출제되는 거의 모든 문제와 답은 패러프레이징되어 있으므로, 문제의 키워드를 파악하고 올바른 정답을 고르기 위해서는 패러프레이징을 익혀두어야 합니다. 한 단어부터 시작해 한 문장, 한 단락 전체가 어떻게 패러프레이징되는지 많이 보고 익숙해지면 쉽게 정답을 파악할 수 있습니다.

> **Paraphrasing의 종류**

(1) 대체 표현을 사용하는 Paraphrasing

원래 문장에서 쓰인 단어를 유의어로 바꾸거나, 표현을 비슷한 의미의 다른 어구로 바꾸거나, 반의어를 사용한 어구로 바꾸어 표현하는 방법입니다. 평소에 어휘 학습을 하면서 유의어나 반의어를 함께 암기해두면, 이러한 paraphrasing을 이해하는 데 도움이 됩니다.

> 예 noted for ~로 유명한 → best known for ~로 유명한 (유의어)
>
> culinary innovations 음식 혁신 → creative dishes 창의적인 요리 (대체 표현)
>
> unpredictable 예측 불가능한 → not anticipated 예상치 못한 (not + 반의어)

(2) 문장 구조를 변경하는 Paraphrasing

원래 문장의 구조를 변경하는 방법입니다. 문장의 성분을 바꾸거나, 능동태를 수동태로 바꾸거나, 일부 문장 성분을 생략하는 등 다양한 paraphrasing의 방식이 있습니다.

> 예 socially determined meanings 사회적으로 결정된 의미
>
> → defined by socially constructed meanings 사회적으로 만들어진 의미에 의해 정의되는 (문장 성분 변경)
>
> several towns were submerged 몇몇 마을들이 수몰되었다
>
> → completely covered many towns 많은 마을들을 완전히 덮었다 (수동태 ↔ 능동태)

(3) 긴 내용을 짧게 요약한 Paraphrasing

원래 문장의 긴 내용을 짧은 표현으로 요약하는 방법입니다.

> 예 is much longer than it once was 한때 그랬던 것보다 훨씬 길다 → has lengthened 길어졌다
>
> in the years following her marriage 결혼 후 수년 뒤에 → after her marriage 결혼 이후

수준별 **맞춤 학습 플랜**

* 진단고사(p.23~31)를 마친 후 결과에 맞는 학습 플랜을 선택하여 공부합니다.

📅 2주 완성 학습 플랜 맞은 개수 10개 이상

	Day 1	Day 2	Day 3	Day 4	Day 5	Day 6	Day 7
Week 1	진단 & 문제 유형 공략하기	PART 1 학습 & HP 풀이	PART 1 HT 풀이	PART 2 학습 & HP 풀이	PART 2 HT 풀이	PART 1~2 리뷰	PART 3 학습 & HP 풀이
Week 2	PART 3 HT 풀이	PART 4 학습 & HP 풀이	PART 4 HT 풀이	PART 3~4 리뷰	실전 1 풀이 & 리뷰	실전 2 풀이 & 리뷰	실전 3 풀이 & 리뷰

📅 3주 완성 학습 플랜 맞은 개수 10개 미만

	Day 1	Day 2	Day 3	Day 4	Day 5	Day 6	Day 7
Week 1	진단 & 문제 유형 공략하기	PART 1 학습 & HP 풀이	PART 1 HT 풀이	PART 1 리뷰	PART 2 학습 & HP 풀이	PART 2 HT 풀이	PART 2 리뷰
Week 2	PART 3 학습 & HP 풀이	PART 3 HT 풀이	PART 3 리뷰	PART 4 학습 & HP 풀이	PART 4 HT 풀이	PART 4 리뷰	휴식
Week 3	실전 1 풀이	실전 1 리뷰	실전 2 풀이	실전 2 리뷰	실전 3 풀이	실전 3 리뷰	전체 리뷰

* 진단: 진단고사   HP: HACKERS PRACTICE   HT: HACKERS TEST   실전: 실전모의고사

학습 플랜 활용법

1. 학습 플랜에 따라 파트별 설명 및 예문을 꼼꼼하게 읽습니다.

2. 문제를 풀 때는 앞에서 배운 학습 내용을 적용시켜 푸는 연습을 합니다.

3. 문제 풀이 직후, 틀린 문제와 헷갈렸던 문제는 반드시 해설을 통해 어느 부분에서 잘못 풀었는지를 확인하고, 다시 한번 풀어봅니다.

4. 파트별 리뷰를 통해 각 파트에서 취약한 부분을 파악하고 보완합니다.

5. 파트별 리뷰를 하는 날은 모르는 단어와 패러프레이징된 표현들을 정리하고 암기합니다.

6. 부록의 유의어 리스트를 매일 자투리 시간을 활용하여 암기합니다.

지텔프·공무원·세무사·취업 시험정보 및 학습자료

Hackers.co.kr

2주 만에 끝내는 **해커스 지텔프 독해 Level 2**

진단고사

실제 지텔프 독해 영역과 유사한 진단고사를 통해 자신의 실력을 평가해보고,
자신에게 맞는 학습 플랜(p.20~21)에 따라 본 교재를 학습하세요.

PIERRE-AUGUSTE RENOIR

Pierre-Auguste Renoir was a French artist who is best known for his role in developing a radical, instinctive painting style known as Impressionism. This style, which liberated painting from strict realism, made him one of the most celebrated artists of the late 19th century.

Renoir was born in 1841 to a family of artisans. From an early age, he showed a fondness for painting and, in 1862, joined Paris's National School of Fine Arts. There he met a group of like-minded artists, including Claude Monet, who shared his love of painting outdoors and using vibrant colors. They were inspired by the quick and spontaneous style of painting practiced by Édouard Manet. Together they created what came to be known as Impressionism.

The mainstream art world initially rejected the works of these painters and criticized them for their messiness. However, the public appreciated the artists and they gradually accumulated a following. In 1876, Renoir painted *Dance at Le Moulin de la Galette*, his most renowned Impressionist work. It perfectly demonstrates Impressionism's distinctive elements. Small, thin brushstrokes evoke the effect of sunlight, creating a luminous effect that mimics the way light changes over time.

Although Renoir was one of the original Impressionists, by the 1880s he had moved on from the style. One reason for this was his commitment to painting portraits of men and women, which required less spontaneity. Nevertheless, he painted many well-known pieces during this period.

Toward the end of his career, Renoir's work was highly acclaimed, and his paintings were hung in the Louvre. Although he suffered from arthritis later in life, he remained productive until his death in 1919.

1. What is Renoir best known for?

    (a) naming a new art movement
    (b) introducing a new brush style
    (c) contributing to a new art style
    (d) becoming a great realist painter

2. Why was Manet's work inspirational to Renoir?

    (a) because Manet used bright colors
    (b) because Manet was committed to outdoor painting
    (c) because Manet employed small brush strokes
    (d) because Manet had a fast and unplanned style

3. What did Renoir accomplish in 1876?

    (a) being accepted by the Paris art world
    (b) exhibiting the first Impressionist work
    (c) moving on from Impressionism
    (d) finishing his most famous Impressionist work

4. Based on the passage, why most likely did Renoir abandon Impressionism?

    (a) He was painting more pictures of people.
    (b) He didn't want to paint portraits anymore.
    (c) He rejected the use of vibrant color.
    (d) He wanted to get his work in the Louvre.

5. In the context of the passage, accumulated means _____.

    (a) gathered
    (b) possessed
    (c) absorbed
    (d) concentrated

PAPER BOTTLES PROVIDE AN ECO-FRIENDLY PACKAGING OPTION

Ecologic Brands, a California-based packaging solutions company, is collaborating with cosmetics company L'Oréal to introduce a reliable, paper-based alternative to the plastic bottle. Its aim is to reduce dependency on plastic bottles and utilize surpluses of recyclable material.

The bottles are made from old newspapers and cardboard, pressed and formed into a firm outer shell. Within this shell, there is a second, inner shell made from 80 percent consumer plastic waste. Overall, the new bottle requires 60 percent less plastic than a regular shampoo or cosmetic bottle.

There are other advantages besides these. First, the bottles themselves can be recycled up to seven times. Second, they have the potential to store a wide range of dry and liquid substances. Third, they can be flattened into compact packages and distributed cheaply in mass quantities.

Ecologic's partnership with L'Oréal also demonstrates the viability of innovative, affordable, and sustainable solutions to environmental problems. Most of the raw material for Ecologic's bottles will come from the waste created in L'Oréal's production of cosmetics. The development of such processes may be one answer to high levels of plastic waste.

To date, Ecologic has prevented 350 tons of plastic from entering landfills and oceans. Currently, one of their main goals is to recycle five tons of L'Oréal's waste each week. Thanks to this pioneering example, other cosmetic companies are <u>examining</u> their use of plastic packaging. Indeed, companies in every industry will start doing so as the issue of plastic waste becomes more acute.

6. What is the article all about?

   (a) a process for recycling plastic
   (b) a replacement for plastic bottles
   (c) a sustainable way of making paper
   (d) a new beauty product line

7. How are Ecologic's bottles manufactured?

   (a) by using discarded cosmetic bottles
   (b) by reusing recycled glass bottles
   (c) by using paper and plastic materials
   (d) by combining natural ingredients

8. According to the article, which of the following is true about Ecologic's bottles?

   (a) They come in seven different sizes.
   (b) They can store dry or wet material.
   (c) They are being shipped overseas.
   (d) They must be purchased in bulk.

9. Where does Ecologic source most of its materials?

   (a) from landfills and garbage dumps
   (b) from the plastic waste in the ocean
   (c) from its employees' discarded substances
   (d) from the waste made in cosmetic production

10. In the context of the passage, <u>examining</u> means _____.

   (a) glimpsing
   (b) challenging
   (c) analyzing
   (d) testing

PART 3. Read the following encyclopedia article and answer the questions. The underlined word in the article is for the vocabulary question.

YOUTUBE

YouTube is a video-sharing website headquartered in San Bruno, California. It was created in 2005 by former PayPal employees Chad Hurley, Steve Chen, and Jawed Karim. They profited from their creation in 2006, when Google acquired it for $1.65 billion.

Originally, YouTube was conceived as a video-hosting dating service, but when that failed to catch on, the site started accepting videos of all kinds. Just a few months later, a Nike video became the first to attract a million views. Within a year, the site was receiving nearly 100 million views a day.

Despite these impressive figures, much of YouTube's early content consisted of amateur videos and clips stolen from TV. When the broadcast network NBC made a highly publicized request that one such clip be taken down, it accidentally helped to make YouTube famous. Shortly thereafter, YouTube reported that they had begun a policy of checking videos for copyright infringement and had partnered with NBC to broadcast licensed content.

YouTube's global audience quickly increased during these early years, with users flocking to the site because it was free and easy to use. Google attempted to monetize this platform by introducing advertisements and offering premium, ad-free services.

YouTube has since spawned an entire industry of content creators who earn shares of YouTube's ad revenue. It has become an essential tool for individuals and entities to communicate, promote, educate, and entertain. Currently, it is ranked by Alexa Internet as the second-most popular site after Google itself.

11. How did YouTube's founders benefit from their site?

(a) by selling stock options for YouTube
(b) by being offered top positions at PayPal
(c) by selling their website to Google
(d) by offering a paid service plan

12. What can be said about YouTube following the launch of the Nike video?

(a) It was mainly being used by sportswear companies.
(b) It was having difficulty gaining an audience.
(c) It was broadcasting many sports games.
(d) It was able to become successful quickly.

13. How did NBC help to make YouTube well-known?

(a) by suing YouTube for copyright infringement
(b) by requesting that YouTube remove a video
(c) by being among YouTube's first-ever advertisers
(d) by losing some of its executives to YouTube

14. Based on the article, which is true about YouTube's content creators?

(a) They exclusively feature educational content.
(b) They do not make their videos for profit.
(c) They make advertisements on YouTube.
(d) They take a portion of YouTube's ad income.

15. In the context of the passage, reported means _____.

(a) announced
(b) argued
(c) testified
(d) overstated

May 21, 2022

Mr. Rogelio Mencia
HR Manager
Banner Medical Center
234 Pecos Road
Chandler, Arizona

Dear Mr. Mencia:

I saw an advertisement on your website for a part-time receptionist at your medical center and I am writing to apply for the job.

I have five years of related experience with businesses throughout Chandler. At my previous job as an administrative assistant for Ainsley Clinic, my responsibilities included managing schedules, processing payments, and dealing with patients' concerns.

At the clinic, I also worked shifts at the reception desk, where I learned the importance of maintaining a strict schedule and communicating clearly and politely with patients. I hope this will demonstrate that I have the necessary skills and experience for the role.

I had taken a three-year break from working to look after my children full time, but they are now old enough that I can return to the workforce.

My attached résumé contains further details about my professional and academic background. I have also included a reference from my last employer. Thank you for this opportunity and I look forward to meeting you.

Sincerely,
Marian Beebe
13 Flint Street
Chandler, Arizona

16. What is the purpose of Marian Beebe's letter to Mr. Mencia?

    (a) to inquire about a receptionist
    (b) to apply for an open position
    (c) to share her family experiences
    (d) to hire a new staff member

17. What kind of work did Marian Beebe do at Ainsley Clinic?

    (a) She arranged patients' prescriptions.
    (b) She contacted patients on the phone.
    (c) She oversaw scheduling for the clinic.
    (d) She managed the company accounts.

18. Why most likely does Ms. Beebe mention her children?

    (a) to explain a brief gap in her career
    (b) to demonstrate her organizational abilities
    (c) to show she has experience working with kids
    (d) to draw attention to her academic background

19. What did Ms. Beebe enclose with her letter?

    (a) samples of her previous work
    (b) a recommendation from Banner Medical Center staff
    (c) certificates from a medical program
    (d) a reference from Ainsley Clinic

20. In the context of the passage, concerns means _____.

    (a) reports
    (b) issues
    (c) proposals
    (d) duties

정답·해석·해설 p.2
· 채점 후 자신에게 맞는 학습 플랜(p.20~21)에 따라 학습하세요.

지텔프·공무원·세무사·취업 시험정보 및 학습자료

Hackers.co.kr

G-TELP 독해
문제 유형 공략하기

지텔프 독해 영역에서는 총 5개의 문제 유형이 출제된다. 각 유형마다 질문 형태 및 단서의 위치가
다르므로 각각에 맞는 문제 풀이 핵심 전략을 적용하면 보다 효율적으로 문제를 풀 수 있다.

1. 주제/목적 문제
2. 특정세부사항 문제
3. Not/True 문제
4. 추론 문제
5. 어휘 문제

① 주제/목적 문제

주제/목적 문제는 지문의 주제나 목적을 정확하게 파악하고 있는지를 확인하는 문제이다. 주제 문제는 PART 2와 PART 3에서 주로 출제되며, 목적 문제는 PART 4에서만 출제된다.

■ 빈출 질문 유형

글의 주제	**What is the article (mainly) about?** 기사는 (주로) 무엇에 대한 것인가? **What is the main subject of the article?** 기사의 중심 주제는 무엇인가? **What is the main topic of the magazine article?** 잡지 기사의 중심 주제는 무엇인가?
글의 목적	**What is the main purpose of the letter?** 편지의 주목적은 무엇인가? **Why is Ms. Kim writing to Mr. Murphy?** Ms. Kim은 왜 Mr. Murphy에게 편지를 쓰고 있는가? **Why did Ms. Stark write a letter to Mr. Johnson?** Ms. Stark는 왜 Mr. Johnson에게 편지를 썼는가?

■ 핵심 전략

제목과 지문의 초반을 스캐닝하라!

주제/목적 문제는 제목이나 지문의 초반에서 주로 정답의 단서를 찾을 수 있다. 특히 PART 2에서는 제목을 통해 주제 문제를 풀 수 있는 경우가 많다.

예제

PART 2

연구가 독감 증세에 대한
습도의 역할을 조사하다

연구는 낮은 습도가 세 가지 다른 방식으로 독감 감염을 이겨낼 면역 체계의 기능에 영향을 미칠 수 있다는 것을 알아냈다. 이 발견은 추운 기온, 낮은 습도, 그리고 독감 사이의 이전에 확인된 관계를 뒷받침하는 데 도움이 된다. 연구는 예일대학교의 연구원들에 의해 시행되었으며 「미국 국립과학원 회보」에 실렸다.
(생략)

기사의 주제는 무엇인가?

(a) 각 계절 동안 독감 전염병이 어떻게 확산하는지
(b) 온도와 습도가 어떻게 감염의 확산을 증가시키는지
(c) 낮은 습도 환경이 어떻게 면역 체계에 영향을 미치는지
(d) 연구원들이 어떻게 독감 치료법을 연구하고 있는지

STUDY EXAMINES ROLE OF HUMIDITY IN FLU CONDITIONS

A study has found that low humidity can affect the immune system's ability to fight flu infections in three different ways. This finding helps to support previously identified links between cold temperatures, low humidity, and the flu. The study was conducted by researchers at Yale University and published in the *Proceedings of the National Academy of Sciences*.
(생략)

What is the article **mainly about**?

(a) how flu infections spread during different seasons
(b) how temperature and humidity increase the spread of infections
(c) how conditions of low humidity affect the immune system
(d) how researchers are investigating flu treatments

• 주제 문제임을 확인한다.

• 제목과 지문의 초반을 스캐닝한다.

examine v. 조사하다 role n. 역할 humidity n. 습도 flu n. 독감 condition n. 증세, 환경 immune adj. 면역의 infection n. 감염, 전염병 identify v. 확인하다 conduct v. 시행하다

해설 제목의 '연구가 독감 증세에 대한 습도의 역할을 조사하다'와 지문 초반의 '낮은 습도가 세 가지 다른 방식으로 면역 체계의 기능에 영향을 미칠 수 있다'라는 단서를 통해, 지문이 낮은 습도 환경이 어떻게 면역 체계에 영향을 미치는지에 대해 이야기할 것임을 알 수 있다. 따라서 (c)가 정답이다.

② 특정세부사항 문제

특정세부사항 문제는 무엇이, 언제, 어떻게, 누가 등 글의 세부 내용에 대해 제대로 파악하고 있는지를 확인하는 문제로, 가장 많이 출제되는 문제 유형이다.

■ 빈출 질문 유형

What	**What** is David Bowie best known for? 데이비드 보위는 무엇으로 가장 유명한가?
Why	**Why** is lemon water considered to be healthy water? 레몬 물은 왜 건강한 물이라고 여겨지는가?
How	**How** is D. Rich trying to prove that its product will be effective? D. Rich 사는 어떻게 그것의 제품이 효과가 있을 것임을 증명하려고 하는가?
When	**When** did Manu Ginobili start playing basketball? 마누 지노빌리는 언제 농구를 하기 시작했는가?
Where	**Where** did Broken Bow Lake get its name from? 브로큰 보우 호수는 어디에서 그 이름을 갖게 되었는가?
Who	**Who** should Mr. Timberg hire before the event? Mr. Timberg는 행사 전에 누구를 고용해야 하는가?

■ 핵심 전략

지문에서 질문의 키워드를 찾아라!

특정세부사항 문제는 질문의 적절한 키워드를 파악하고, 이를 지문에서 찾아내는 것이 핵심이다. 세부적인 내용을 묻기 때문에 키워드의 주변 내용을 주의 깊게 읽으면 쉽게 정답을 찾을 수 있다. 정답은 일반적으로 지문의 내용이 그대로 언급되어 있거나 paraphrasing된 형태이다.

예제

PART 1

마사 그레이엄	**MARTHA GRAHAM**
(생략)	(생략)
그녀가 14살이었을 때, 그레이엄은 그녀의 가족과 함께 캘리포니아 주의 산타바바라로 이주했다. 17살 때, 그녀는 유명한 현대 무용 개척자인 루스 세인트 데니스가 메이슨 오페라 하우스에서 공연하는 것을 보았는데, 이는 그녀가 무용에 경력을 추구하도록 영감을 주었다. 그레이엄은 그 다음 해에 세인트 데니스의 데니숀 무용학교에 입학했다.	When she was 14, Graham moved with her family to Santa Barbara, California. At 17, she watched noted modern dance pioneer Ruth St. Denis perform at the Mason Opera House, which inspired her to pursue a career in dancing . Graham enrolled in St. Denis's Denishawn School of Dancing and Related Arts the following year.
(생략)	(생략)

● 특정세부사항 문제임을 확인한다.

● 지문에서 질문의 키워드 wanted to be a dancer를 찾는다.

그레이엄은 언제 무용가가 되고 싶다고 결심했는가?	**When** did Graham decide that she wanted to be a dancer ?
(a) 학교 무용 공연에 참여한 후에	(a) after joining a dance performance at school
(b) 유명한 무용가가 공연하는 것을 본 후에	(b) after watching a famous dancer perform
(c) 산타바바라의 본가를 떠난 후에	(c) after leaving her family home in Santa Barbara
(d) 메이슨 오페라 하우스에서 일한 후에	(d) after working at the Mason Opera House

noted adj. 유명한 modern adj. 현대의, 근대의 pioneer n. 개척자, 선구자 perform v. 공연하다, 연기하다
inspire v. 영감을 주다 pursue v. 추구하다 career n. 경력 enroll v. 입학하다, 등록하다

해설 질문의 키워드가 pursue a career in dancing으로 paraphrasing된 주변 내용을 주의 깊게 읽으면, '마사 그레이엄이 유명한 무용가 루스 세인트 데니스가 공연하는 것을 보았고, 이것이 그녀가 무용에 경력을 추구하도록 영감을 주었다'고 했다. 따라서 (b)가 정답이다.

❸ Not/True 문제

Not/True 문제는 지문 내용을 바탕으로 보기 4개 중 틀린 것 또는 옳은 것을 골라냄으로써 세부 내용을 정확히 이해하고 있는지를 확인하는 문제이다. 보통 1~3개씩 출제되지만 간혹 출제되지 않기도 하는 문제 유형이다.

■ 빈출 질문 유형

Not 문제	**What is not one of the treatments?** 치료법 중 하나가 아닌 것은 무엇인가? **What does NOT describe sinkholes?** 싱크홀을 설명하는 것이 아닌 것은 무엇인가? **Which does not affect people's bad impressions?** 사람의 나쁜 인상에 영향을 미치는 것이 아닌 것은 무엇인가?
True 문제	**What is true about northern lights?** 북극광에 대해 사실인 것은 무엇인가? **Which statement is true about photosynthesis?** 광합성에 대해 사실인 설명은 무엇인가?

■ 핵심 전략

각 보기와 지문 내용을 하나씩 대조하라!

Not/True 문제는 각 보기와 지문 내용을 하나씩 대조하여 정답을 선택해야 한다. 문제가 묻는 것이 무엇인지 확인한 뒤, 관련된 부분에서 각 보기의 키워드가 언급된 주변 내용을 주의 깊게 읽어야 한다. Not 문제는 지문의 내용과 일치하지 않거나 아예 지문에 언급되지 않은 것이 정답이며, True 문제는 지문의 내용이 그대로 언급되거나 paraphrasing된 것이 정답이다.

예제

PART 3

거인이 만든 길	**GIANT'S CAUSEWAY**
(생략)	(생략)
거인이 만든 길은 북아일랜드를 스코틀랜드에 연결하는 길, 즉 둑길을 만들기 위해 이 구성물을 지은 거인에 대한 허구의 이야기에서 이름의 유래를 찾는다. 실제로는, 그 기둥들은 5천만 년에서 6천만 년 전에 일어난 장기적인 화산 활동의 결과로, 이때 해수면으로 밀려온 용암이 잇따른 층으로 식은 것이다.	Giant's Causeway **derives its name** from the **fictional story** of a giant who **built** the formation to form a road, or causeway, connecting Northern Ireland to Scotland. In reality, the columns are the result of prolonged **volcanic activity** that occurred about 50 to 60 million years ago, when lava pushed to the **surface** was cooled in successive layers.
(생략)	(생략)
거인이 만든 길에 대해 사실인 것은?	Which is **true** about the Giant's Causeway?
(a) 허구적인 사건에서 이름을 얻는다.	(a) It **gets its name** from a fictional event.
(b) 화산 활동에 의해 파괴되었다.	(b) It was destroyed by a **volcanic eruption** .
(c) 수송을 목적으로 지어졌다.	(c) It was **built** for the purpose of transport.
(d) 주로 해수면 아래에 있다.	(d) It is mainly under the **surface of the water** .

• **True** 문제임을 확인한다.

• 각 보기와 지문 내용을 하나씩 대조한다.

derive v. 유래를 찾다 **fictional** adj. 허구의 **formation** n. 구성물 **column** n. 기둥 **prolonged** adj. 장기적인 **occur** v. 일어나다 **successive** adj. 잇따른, 연속적인 **layer** n. 층

해설 보기 (a)의 키워드 gets its name이 derives its name으로 paraphrasing된 주변 내용을 주의 깊게 읽으면, '허구의 이야기에서 Giant's Causeway의 이름의 유래를 찾는다'고 했다. 따라서 (a)가 정답이다. 보기 (b)는 기둥들이 화산 활동의 결과라고 했으므로 오답이다. 보기 (c)는 허구의 이야기라고 했으므로 오답이다. 보기 (d)는 해수면으로 밀려왔다고 했으므로 오답이다.

④ 추론 문제

추론 문제는 지문의 내용을 근거로 새로운 사실을 추론할 수 있는지를 확인하는 문제이다. 지문 일부만을 단서로 하여 세부적인 내용을 추론하는 문제가 많이 출제되는데, 직접적인 단서가 언급되지는 않으므로 지문의 내용을 정확히 이해하고 올바른 추론을 해야 한다. 보통 5~7개씩 출제되는 문제 유형이다.

▇ 빈출 질문 유형

What **probably** happened to the earlier investment?
초기 투자에 무슨 일이 일어났던 것 같은가?

Why **most likely** do people tend to follow what others do?
왜 사람들은 다른 사람들이 하는 것을 따라 하려는 경향이 있는 것 같은가?

Which **can be** expected during the special event on July 7?
7월 7일 특별 행사에서 무엇이 기대될 수 있는가?

▇ 핵심 전략

반드시 질문의 키워드가 언급된 주변 내용을 토대로 가장 적절히 추론한 보기를 찾아라!

추론 문제는 지문에 직접적인 정답의 단서가 없으므로 까다로운 문제로 여겨질 수 있다. 하지만 지문에서 질문의 키워드가 언급된 주변 내용을 읽고, 이를 토대로 4개 보기 중 가장 적절한 추론을 한 보기를 찾으면 어렵지 않게 정답을 찾을 수 있다. 이때, 지문에서 언급되지 않은 일반 상식을 통해 추론할 수 있는 내용을 정답으로 선택하지 않도록 주의해야 한다.

예제

PART 4

Netshop 고객 서비스
Netshop 주식회사
12201 뉴욕 주

관련분께,

(생략)

이것은 단순히 용납할 수 없습니다.
이 편지와 함께 동봉된 것은 제 주문
의 손상된 상품을 찍은 사진입니다.
저는 영수증의 사본과 함께 이것을
Netshop 사로 반품하려고 준비하
고 있습니다. 반품 방침에 명시된 대
로, 저는 이것이 추가 금액 없이 즉시
교체될 것이라고 믿습니다.

(생략)

Philip Lindsay 드림

Netshop 사는 이 편지에 대한 대응
으로 무엇을 할 것 같은가?

(a) 반품 방침을 확인하는 것을 제
    안할 것이다.
(b) Philip에게 그의 주문 금액을 환
    불해줄 것이다.
(c) 상품의 사진을 요청할 것이다.
(d) 이전 것을 받은 후 새 상품을 발
    송할 것이다.

Netshop Customer Services
Netshop Inc.
New York State, 12201

To Whom It May Concern,

(생략)

This is simply unacceptable. Enclosed with
this letter are photographs I have taken of the
damaged items from my order. I am preparing
to send them back to Netshop along with
a copy of my receipt. I trust that they will be
replaced immediately and at no additional cost
to me, as your return policy suggests.

(생략)

Sincerely,
Philip Lindsay

What will Netshop probably do as a response
to this letter?

(a) It will suggest checking the return policy.
(b) It will send Philip a refund for the cost of his
    order.
(c) It will request photos of the items.
(d) It will ship new items after receiving the old
    ones.

● 추론 문제임을 확인한다.

● 질문의 키워드가 언급된
  주변 내용을 토대로 가
  장 적절히 추론한 보기를
  찾는다.

---

unacceptable adj. 용납할 수 없는 enclose v. 동봉하다 receipt n. 영수증 replace v. 교체하다 policy n. 방침, 정책

해설 질문의 키워드 Netshop이 언급된 주변 내용을 주의 깊게 읽으면, 'Philip Lindsay가 상품을 반품하려고 하며 반품 방침에 명
시된 대로 이것이 교체될 것이라고 믿는다'고 했다. 이를 토대로 Netshop이 이전 상품을 받은 후 새 상품을 발송할 것임을 추
론할 수 있다. 따라서 (d)가 정답이다.

⑤ 어휘 문제

어휘 문제는 지문에 밑줄로 표시되어 있는 어휘의 문맥상 유의어를 고르는 문제이다. 한 파트당 2문제씩, 총 8문제가 고정적으로 출제되므로 중요도가 높은 문제 유형이다.

■ 빈출 질문 유형

In the context of the passage, expand means _____.
지문의 문맥에서, 'expand'는 –을 의미한다.

■ 핵심 전략

어휘가 사용된 문맥을 파악하라!

주어진 어휘가 사용된 문맥의 내용을 정확히 파악하고 어휘가 무슨 뜻으로 사용되었는지를 파악하는 것이 중요하다. 사전적 유의어라고 해도 문맥에서 사용된 것과 의미가 다를 수 있기 때문에 암기한 유의어를 무조건적으로 정답으로 선택하지 않도록 주의한다. 최근에는 보기에 유의어가 2개 이상 주어지는 경우와 사전적 유의어가 아니어도 지문의 문맥에서 의미하는 뜻을 가진 어휘가 정답인 경우가 많아지고 있다.

2개 이상의 유의어가 주어지는 경우

> They should make sure the students perform well in class. Students' performance will be reflected in their grades.
>
> In the context of the passage, perform means _____.
>
> (a) do   (b) satisfy   (c) act   (d) transfer
>
> ➡ perform의 유의어인 do와 act가 모두 보기에 주어질 수 있다. 이때, 위 문장은 학생들이 수업에서 잘 하는지 확인해야 하며 그것이 학생들의 성적에 반영될 것이라는 뜻이므로, perform이 '하다'라는 의미로 사용되는 것이 더 자연스럽다. 따라서 (a) do가 정답이다. 'act well'은 '연기를 잘하다', '맡은 역할을 해내다'와 같은 의미로 사용되므로 자연스럽지 않다.

사전적 유의어가 아니어도 지문의 문맥에서 의미하는 뜻이 되는 경우

> I think you should solve this problem as soon as possible. It is a major issue that must be fixed.
>
> In the context of the passage, solve means _____.
>
> (a) correct   (b) fulfill   (c) reach   (d) promote
>
> ➡ solve의 사전적 의미는 '해결하다', '풀다'이며 동의어로는 resolve, work out 등이 있다. 하지만 위 문장은 가능한 한 빨리 문제를 고쳐야 한다는 뜻이므로, solve가 '문제를 고치다'라는 의미로 사용된 것을 알 수 있다. 따라서 (a) correct가 사전적 유의어가 아니어도 정답이 된다.

■ 예제

PART 3

<table>
<tr>
<td>

「모든 것이 무너져 내리다」

(생략)

1958년에, 「모든 것이 무너져 내리다」의 완성된 원고는 런던의 여러 출판사에 보내졌는데, 그들은 모두 아프리카인 작가의 작품은 팔리지 않을 것이라는 신념으로 이를 거절했다. 하지만, 하이네만 사에서, 최근에 아프리카에서 돌아온 한 상담가가 이 소설은 그가 수년 동안 읽었던 것 중 최고이니 이 작품을 출판하라고 설득했다.

(생략)

</td>
<td>

Things Fall Apart

(생략)

In 1958, the completed manuscript for *Things Fall Apart* was sent to several publishers in London, all of whom rejected it in the belief that books by African writers did not sell. However, at Heinemann, a consultant recently returned from Africa persuaded the company to publish the work by declaring it the best novel he had read in years.

(생략)

</td>
</tr>
<tr>
<td>

지문의 문맥에서, 'persuaded'는 –을 의미한다.

(a) 안심시켰다
(b) 설득했다
(c) 단념시켰다
(d) 양육했다

</td>
<td>

In the context of the passage, persuaded means _____.

(a) satisfied
(b) convinced
(c) deterred
(d) nurtured

</td>
</tr>
</table>

• 어휘 문제임을 확인한다.

• 어휘가 사용된 문맥을 파악한다.

manuscript n. 원고 **reject** v. 거절하다 **belief** n. 신념 **consultant** n. 상담가 **persuade** v. 설득하다

해설 지문에서 persuaded가 포함되어 있는 문장을 보면, '출판사에서 한 상담가가 이 소설은 수년 동안 읽었던 것 중 최고이니 출판하라고 설득했다'고 했다. (a) satisfied도 persuaded의 유의어지만 문맥상 '최고의 책이라고 말하며 책을 출판하도록 안심시켰다'보다는 '설득했다'는 내용이 더 자연스러우므로 '설득했다'라는 의미의 (b) convinced가 정답이다.

PART
1

인물의 일대기

Biographical/Historical Article

PART 1 인물의 일대기 Biographical/Historical Article

PART 1에서는 특정 인물의 일대기를 시간 순서대로 서술하는 지문이 출제된다. 4개 파트 중에서 가장 흐름이 고정적인 지문 유형이며, 시기별로 중요한 사건 및 업적을 묻는 문제가 주로 출제된다.

-○ 출제 토픽

역사적 위인이나 근현대의 유명한 인물이 주로 출제된다. 기존에는 과거의 위인이나 역사적 인물들이 많이 출제되는 편이었으나, 최근에는 우리에게 친숙한 동시대의 유명 인사들도 많이 등장하는 편이다.

· 예술가	프린스(가수), 스티븐 스필버그(영화 감독), 캐리 피셔(영화 배우), 라파엘로 산치오(화가)	
· 운동선수	마이클 펠프스(수영 선수), 미셸 콴(피겨스케이팅 선수), 리오넬 메시(축구 선수)	
· 과거의 위인	나폴레옹 보나파르트(프랑스 황제), 오스카 쉰들러(유대인 구출에 기여한 독일 사업가)	
· 기타	커밋(TV 프로그램 캐릭터), 안나 윈투어(보그 편집장)	

-○ 문제 유형

특정세부사항 문제가 가장 많이 출제되는 파트이며, 첫 문제는 주로 인물이 유명한 이유를 묻는다. 주제/목적 문제는 출제되지 않는다.

특정세부사항	인물이 유명한 이유, 진로를 정한 계기, 시기별로 인물이 한 일 등의 세부사항을 묻는다. **What** is Watson most famous for? 왓슨은 무엇으로 가장 유명한가?
Not/True	인물에 대해 언급된 사건 등에 대해 사실이거나 사실이 아닌 것을 묻는다. Which is **true** about Alfred Vail's childhood? 알프레드 베일의 어린 시절에 대해 사실인 것은?
추론	인물에게 일어난 사건 등에 대해 추론할 수 있는 것을 묻는다. Why **most likely** did Vincent van Gogh have to repeat a year at the academy? 왜 빈센트 반 고흐는 아카데미에서 유급이 되어야 했던 것 같은가?
어휘	지문의 문맥에서 밑줄 어휘의 유의어가 무엇인지를 묻는다. In the context of the passage, expand means _____. 지문의 문맥에서, 'expand'는 ~을 의미한다.

-○ 핵심 전략

1. '인물 소개 → 어린 시절 → 주요 활동 → 근황 또는 죽음'의 패턴화된 흐름에서 출제되는 빈출 문제들을 알아두어야 한다.

2. 유명한 이유, 시기별 활동, 진로 선택 계기 등을 설명하는 내용은 관련 표현을 익혀두면 쉽게 찾을 수 있다.

3. 질문의 고유명사와 숫자는 보통 paraphrasing되지 않으므로, 이를 키워드로 잡으면 지문에서 단서를 쉽게 찾을 수 있다.

지문 흐름별 빈출 문제

고든 램지

고든 램지는 불같은 성격으로 유명한 영국의 스타 셰프이자, 작가, 방송인, 음식 평론가이다. 그는 1990년대 말에 방송에 출연하면서 가장 영향력 있는 셰프 중 한 명이 되었다.

고든 램지는 1966년 11월 8일에 스코틀랜드 렌프루셔에서 4남매 중 둘째로 태어났다. 12살부터 19살까지 유망한 축구 선수로 활약하기도 했지만, 잦은 부상으로 인해 그만둬야 했다. 부모님의 이혼과 우울한 생활 속에서 램지는 요리를 하면서 즐거움을 찾기 시작했다.

1980년대 중반에 램지는 록스턴 하우스 호텔에서 부주방장으로 일하면서 본격적으로 요리 경력을 시작했다. 이후, 그는 런던으로 이주하여 마르코 피에르 화이트 밑에서 일하면서 요리를 제대로 배울 수 있었다. 2년 10개월 동안 그의 밑에서 일한 뒤, 램지는 프랑스 음식을 공부하고자 했고 알버트 루라는 프랑스 요리사 밑에서 일하게 되었다.

이후 그는 23살의 나이에 파리로 가서 미슐랭 별을 받은 두 명의 셰프인 기 사부아와 조엘 로부숑과 일하게 되었다. 이후 이탈리아에서, 그리고 다시 런던에서 경력을 쌓아 나가다가 1998년에 드디어 자신의 레스토랑을 개업했고, 2001년에 세 번째 미슐랭 별을 받으며 승승장구했다. 램지는 그 이후 더 많은 레스토랑을 개업하고 세계적으로 유명해졌다.

램지는 자선 사업에도 힘쓰고 있다. 유니세프에서 주관하는 자선 축구 경기인 사커에이드 행사에는 단 한 번도 빠지지 않고 참가하기도 했다. 이렇게, 방송에서 주로 보여주는 불같은 성격 외에도 친절하고 사려 깊은 사람이기도 하다.

지문 흐름 | 흐름에 따른 빈출 문제

인물 소개

유명한 이유를 묻는 문제가 주로 출제된다.
ex What is Ramsay most famous for?
램지는 무엇으로 가장 유명한가?

어린 시절 및 진로 선택 계기

진로 선택 계기를 묻는 문제가 주로 출제된다.
ex What made Ramsay start cooking?
무엇이 램지가 요리를 하기 시작하도록 했는가?

어린 시절에 관한 세부사항을 묻는 문제가 출제된다.
ex Which is true about Gordon Ramsay's childhood?
램지의 어린 시절에 대해 사실인 것은?

활동 시작 및 청년 시절

처음 시작한 활동 등을 묻는 문제가 주로 출제된다.
ex How did Ramsay's cooking career get launched?
램지의 요리 경력은 어떻게 시작되었는가?

초기 활동에 관한 세부사항을 묻는 문제가 출제된다.
ex Who made it possible for Ramsay to learn more about cuisine?
램지가 요리에 대해 제대로 배울 수 있도록 한 것은 누구였는가?

주요 활동 및 업적

주요 활동에 관한 세부사항을 묻는 문제가 출제된다.
ex When did Ramsay open his first restaurant?
램지는 언제 그의 첫 레스토랑을 개업했는가?

업적에 관해 묻는 문제가 주로 출제된다.
ex What did he accomplish in 2001?
그는 2001년에 무엇을 성취했는가?

인물 평가 및 근황 또는 죽음

인물에 대한 평가를 묻는 문제가 주로 출제된다.
ex What could be said about Gordon Ramsay?
고든 램지에 대해 무엇이라고 말할 수 있는가?

근황이나 죽음에 관해 묻는 문제가 출제된다.
ex How does he currently spend his days?
그는 요즘 어떻게 지내는가?

1. 유명한 이유

① **be best known for**　~으로 가장 잘 알려져 있다

Vincent van Gogh **is best known for** his intense colors and dramatic brushwork.
빈센트 반 고흐는 그의 강렬한 색감과 인상적인 화법으로 가장 잘 알려져 있다.

② **be famous for / be noted for**　~으로 유명하다

Amy Tan is an American writer, who **is famous for** her novels that look at Chinese American experience.
에이미 탄은 미국의 작가로, 중국계 미국인의 삶을 살펴보는 소설들로 유명하다.

③ **be recognized for**　~으로 인정받다

John Lennon **is recognized for** the strong wit in his music.
존 레논은 음악의 강렬한 재치로 인정받는다.

2. 시기

④ **At the age of**　~살 때

At the age of seven, she could already paint impressively lifelike portraits.
7살 때, 그녀는 이미 놀라울 정도로 실물과 똑같은 초상화를 그릴 수 있었다.

⑤ **Since**　~ 이래로

Since 1986, he has disappeared from the industry.
1986년 이래로, 그는 그 산업에서 사라졌다.

⑥ **After -ing**　~한 이후에

After graduating, she became a lawyer at K&J.
졸업을 한 이후에, 그녀는 K&J에서 변호사가 되었다.

3. 진로를 정한 계기

⑦ **inspire 인물 to**　(인물)에게 ~을 하도록 영감을 주다

His father told him about his adventure at sea, and this **inspired him to** become a sailor.
그의 아버지는 자신의 항해 모험담을 말해주었고, 이는 그가 선원이 되도록 영감을 주었다.

⑧ **first show an interest in**　~에 처음 관심을 보이다

She **first showed an interest in** acting during high school.
그녀는 고등학교를 다니던 중에 연기하는 것에 처음 관심을 보였다.

⑨ **be introduced to**　~에게 소개되다

He **was introduced to** Jean-Claude, who became his hotel manager later on.
그는 나중에 그의 호텔 지배인이 된 장 클로드에게 소개되었다.

1. 인물 소개

regard v. ~으로 여기다

pioneer n. 선구자

talented adj. 재능이 있는

influential adj. 영향력 있는

modern adj. 현대적인

essential adj. 필수적인, 가장 중요한

2. 인물의 유년기 · 청년기

be born phr. 태어나다

practice v. 연습하다

undergo v. 경험하다, 견디다

experience n. 경험, 경력 v. 겪다, 경험하다

graduate v. 졸업하다

scholarship n. 장학 제도, 장학금

attend v. 다니다, 참석하다

earn v. 얻다, 벌다

receive v. 받다, 받아들이다

pursue v. 종사하다, 추구하다

impress v. 깊은 인상을 주다

outstanding adj. 뛰어난, 우수한

3. 인물의 활동 · 업적

achievement n. 업적, 성취한 것

prosper v. 번영하다, 번창하다

prefer v. 좋아하다, 선호하다

produce v. 생산하다, 만들다

establish v. 확고히 하다, 설립하다

found v. 설립하다, 만들다

efficient adj. 효율적인, 유능한

develop v. 개발하다, 성장시키다

improve v. 개선하다, 향상시키다

realize v. 깨닫다, 달성하다

notice v. 알아채다, 주목하다

implement v. 시행하다

4. 인물에 대한 평가 · 근황

consider v. (~을 ~으로) 여기다

devote v. (시간 · 노력을) 쏟다, 바치다

dedicate v. 헌정하다, 바치다

charity n. 자선 사업

suffer v. 고통받다, 시달리다, 앓다

resign v. 사임하다, 그만두다

acknowledge v. 인정하다

reputation n. 평판, 명성

JULIE ANDREWS

지문 흐름

1   **Julie Andrews is an English actress and singer** most famous for **the purity and range of her voice.** She attained renown for her roles in two hugely successful films, *Mary Poppins* and *The Sound of Music*.

1번 키워드

인물 소개

2   Andrews was born in Walton-on-Thames, England, in 1935. Her mother was a pianist and her stepfather was a singer, so Andrews was exposed to music from early childhood. Hearing her sing, **her stepfather recognized her talent and paid for her to have singing lessons from Lilian Stiles-Allen, a well-known soprano, which** inspired **her to take up a musical career**.

2번 키워드

어린 시절 및 진로 결정 계기

3   In 1947, she made her professional debut, singing an operatic aria in *Starlight Roof*. And in 1954, **Andrews appeared on Broadway for the first time in the musical *The Boy Friend*, which made her** popular among American audiences. After that, her career steadily progressed, with multiple appearances on American television and roles in the musicals *My Fair Lady* and *Camelot*.

3번 키워드

활동 시작 및 초기 활동

4   Based on her crowd-pleasing performances in musicals, **Andrews was offered her** first film role **in Disney's 1964 movie *Mary Poppins*,** which broke box office records. Following that, she enhanced her place in Hollywood by starring in 1965's *The Sound of Music*, one of the most successful films of all time. These two iconic performances won Andrews multiple awards, including an Oscar and two Golden Globes.

4번 키워드

주요 활동 및 경력의 전환점

5   In the 1970s, **Andrews's career** slowed down **as musicals became less popular.** She was also branded old-fashioned by younger generations. In recent decades, she has revived her career and has starred in profitable commercial films like *The Princess Diaries*.

5번 키워드

인물의 후기 활동 및 근황

유명한 이유를 묻고 있으므로, 인물을 소개하는 1단락에서 단서를 찾는다.

1. What is Julie Andrews famous for ?

   (a) composing hit musicals

   (b) having a good singing voice

   (c) directing successful films

   (d) acting in a range of movie types

경력을 추구하기로 결심한 때를 묻고 있으므로, 진로 결정 계기를 서술하는 2단락에서 단서를 찾는다.

2. When did Andrews decide to pursue a musical career?

   (a) when she moved to the US

   (b) after seeing her mother and stepfather perform

   (c) during her time in *Starlight Roof*

   (d) when she was taught by Lilian Stiles-Allen

미국에서 유명해진 계기를 묻고 있으므로, 질문의 키워드 well known in America가 popular among American audiences로 paraphrasing되어 언급된 3단락에서 단서를 찾는다.

3. Based on the article, how did Andrews become well known in America ?

   (a) by appearing in a musical on Broadway

   (b) by making her cinematic debut

   (c) by winning a Golden Globe

   (d) by starring in *The Sound of Music*

첫 영화 배역을 묻고 있으므로, 질문의 키워드 first movie role이 first film role으로 paraphrasing되어 언급된 4단락에서 단서를 찾는다.

4. Which film featured Andrews in her first movie role ?

   (a) *The Boy Friend*

   (b) *The Sound of Music*

   (c) *My Fair Lady*

   (d) *Mary Poppins*

경력 쇠퇴를 야기했던 것을 묻고 있으므로, 인물의 후기 활동을 서술하는 5단락에서 단서를 찾는다.

5. What most likely led to Andrews's career declining ?

   (a) She retired from acting in musicals.

   (b) She took on roles in commercial movies.

   (c) The tastes of audiences changed.

   (d) Directors wanted younger actresses.

6. In the context of the passage, renown means
   _____ .

   (a) popularity

   (b) notoriety

   (c) knowledge

   (d) profit

7. In the context of the passage, branded means
   _____ .

   (a) fashioned

   (b) marketed

   (c) stamped

   (d) identified

해석 및 해설 뒷장에서 확인하기 ➡

줄리 앤드류스

1 [1]줄리 앤드류스는 목소리의 청아함과 음역대로 가장 유명한 영국의 여배우 겸 가수이다. 그녀는 크게 성공한 두 영화, 「메리 포핀스」와 「사운드 오브 뮤직」에서의 배역으로 명성을 얻었다.

2 앤드류스는 1935년에 영국의 월튼 온 템즈에서 태어났다. 그녀의 어머니는 피아니스트였으며 양아버지는 가수였으므로, 앤드류스는 아주 어릴 때부터 음악을 접했다. 그녀가 노래하는 것을 듣고, [2]그녀의 양아버지는 재능을 알아보고 그녀가 유명한 소프라노 가수인 릴리안 스타일스 알렌에게서 노래 강습을 받을 수 있도록 돈을 지불했고, 이는 그녀가 음악적인 경력을 시작하도록 영감을 주었다.

3 1947년에, 그녀는 「스타라이프 루프」에서 오페라 아리아를 노래하며 프로로 데뷔했다. 그리고 1954년에, [3]앤드류스는 뮤지컬 「보이 프렌드」에서 처음으로 브로드웨이에 출연했고, 이는 그녀가 미국 관중 사이에 인기 있게 만들었다. 그 후, 미국 TV 방송 다수 출연과 뮤지컬 「마이 페어 레이디」와 「카멜롯」의 배역을 통해 그녀의 경력은 안정적으로 진전을 보였다.

4 뮤지컬에서 관객을 만족시키는 그녀의 연기에 기반하여, [4]앤드류스는 디즈니의 1964년 영화 「메리 포핀스」에서 그녀의 첫 영화 배역을 제안받았는데, 이는 영화 흥행 기록을 깼다. 뒤이어, 그녀는 역대 가장 성공적인 영화 중 하나인 1965년 작 「사운드 오브 뮤직」에서 주연을 맡으며 할리우드에서 그녀의 지위를 향상시켰다. 이 두 대표적인 연기는 앤드류스에게 다수의 상을 받도록 했으며, 오스카상과 두 개의 골든 글로브상이 포함된다.

5 1970년대에, [5]앤드류스의 경력은 뮤지컬이 인기가 떨어지면서 부진했다. 그녀는 또한 젊은 세대에게는 구식이라고 단정되기도 했었다. 최근 수십 년간, 그녀는 자신의 경력을 되살려서 「프린세스 다이어리」와 같은 수익성 있는 상업 영화에서 주연을 맡았다.

어휘 **actress** n. 여배우 **purity** n. 청아함, 맑음 **range** n. 음역대, 범위 **attain** v. 얻다, 이루다 **renown** n. 명성
expose v. 접하게 하다, 드러내다 **recognize** v. 알아보다, 인정하다 **pay** v. (돈을) 지불하다 **inspire** v. 영감을 주다, 이끌다
steadily adv. 안정적으로, 꾸준히 **progress** v. 진전을 보이다, 나아가다 **multiple** adj. 다수의, 다양한 **appearance** n. 출연, 겉모습
performance n. 연기, 공연 **break a record** phr. 기록을 깨다 **star** v. 주연을 맡다 **brand** v. 단정하다, 낙인을 찍다
old-fashioned adj. 구식의 **generation** n. 세대 **decade** n. 10년 **revive** v. 되살리다, 부활시키다 **profitable** adj. 수익성 있는
commercial adj. 상업의

1. **특정세부사항** 유명한 이유   정답 (b)

해석 줄리 앤드류스는 무엇으로 유명한가?

  (a) 성공적인 뮤지컬을 작곡한 것

  (b) 좋은 노래하는 목소리를 가진 것

  (c) 성공한 영화를 감독한 것

  (d) 다양한 영화 장르에서 연기한 것

해설 1단락의 'Julie Andrews is ~ most famous for the purity and range of her voice.'에서 줄리 앤드류스는 목소리의 청아함과 음역대로 가장 유명하다고 했다. 따라서 (b)가 정답이다.

2. **특정세부사항** When   정답 (d)

해석 앤드류스는 언제 음악적인 경력을 추구하기로 결심했는가?

  (a) 그녀가 미국으로 이사 갔을 때

  (b) 어머니와 양아버지가 공연하는 것을 본 후에

  (c) 「스타라이프 루프」에서 공연하던 시기 중에

  (d) 릴리안 스타일스 알렌에게 가르침을 받았을 때

해설 2단락의 'her stepfather ~ paid for her to have singing lessons from Lilian Stiles-Allen, ~ which inspired her to take up a musical career'에서 그녀의 양아버지는 그녀가 릴리안 스타일스 알렌에게서 노래 강습을 받을 수 있도록 돈을 지불했고, 이는 그녀가 음악적인 경력을 시작하도록 영감을 주었다고 했다. 따라서 (d)가 정답이다.

3. **특정세부사항** How   정답 (a)

해석 지문에 따르면, 앤드류스는 어떻게 미국에서 잘 알려지게 되었는가?

  (a) 브로드웨이 뮤지컬에 출연함으로써

  (b) 영화 데뷔를 함으로써

  (c) 골든 글로브상을 받음으로써

  (d) 「사운드 오브 뮤직」에서 주연을 맡음으로써

해설 3단락의 'Andrews appeared on Broadway for the first time in the musical ~, which made her popular among American audiences'에서 앤드류스는 뮤지컬에서 처음으로 브로드웨이에 출연했고, 이는 그녀가 미국 관중 사이에 인기 있게 만들었다고 했다. 따라서 (a)가 정답이다.

4. **특정세부사항** Which   정답 (d)

해석 어떤 영화에서 앤드류스의 첫 영화 배역을 선보였는가?

  (a) 「보이프렌드」

  (b) 「사운드 오브 뮤직」

  (c) 「마이 페어 레이디」

  (d) 「메리 포핀스」

해설 4단락의 'Andrews was offered her first film role in Disney's 1964 movie Mary Poppins'에서 앤드류스는 디즈니의 1964년 영화 「메리 포핀스」의 배역으로 그녀의 첫 영화 배역을 제안 받았다고 했다. 따라서 (d)가 정답이다.

5. **추론** 특정사실   정답 (c)

해석 앤드류스의 경력 쇠퇴를 야기했던 것은 무엇일 것 같은가?

  (a) 뮤지컬에서 연기하는 것을 그만두었다.

  (b) 상업 영화들의 배역을 맡았다.

  (c) 관중의 취향이 바뀌었다.

  (d) 감독들이 더 어린 배우를 원했다.

해설 5단락의 'Andrews's career slowed down as musicals became less popular'에서 앤드류스의 경력은 뮤지컬이 인기가 떨어지면서 부진했다고 한 것을 통해, 관중의 취향이 바뀌었음을 추론할 수 있다. 따라서 (c)가 정답이다.

6. **어휘** 유의어   정답 (a)

해석 지문의 문맥에서, 'renown'은 −을 의미한다.

  (a) 인기

  (b) 악평

  (c) 지식

  (d) 이익

해설 1단락의 'She attained renown for her roles in two hugely successful films'는 그녀는 크게 성공한 두 영화에서의 배역으로 '명성'을 얻었다는 뜻이므로, '인기'라는 비슷한 의미의 (a)가 정답이다.

7. **어휘** 유의어   정답 (d)

해석 지문의 문맥에서, 'branded'는 −을 의미한다.

  (a) 만들어졌다

  (b) 내놓였다

  (c) 각인되었다

  (d) 취급되었다

해설 5단락의 'She was ~ branded old-fashioned by younger generations.'는 그녀는 또한 젊은 세대에게는 구식이라고 '단정되었다'는 뜻이므로, '취급되었다'라는 비슷한 의미의 (d)가 정답이다.

지문의 내용을 올바르게 paraphrasing한 것을 고르세요.

01

> Colonel Sanders started the now world-famous KFC chain of fried-chicken restaurants as a humble roadside diner during the Great Depression. His physical features, such as his goatee and white hair, have been used to make him an international icon for the brand.

(a) Colonel Sanders was famous for his fried chicken when he started KFC.
(b) Colonel Sanders grew his restaurant business from a small eatery.

02

> Albert Sabin was an American medical researcher known for his radical work on the oral polio vaccine, which was instrumental in limiting the disease worldwide. Aside from testing the live vaccine on himself, Sabin famously refused to patent it so that it could be widely distributed at an affordable price.

(a) The widespread use of Sabin's vaccine made him a wealthy man.
(b) Sabin worked hard to ensure his vaccine reached more people.

03

> Born in 1643, Isaac Newton was an English scientist known for devising physical laws. His book, *Mathematical Principles of Natural Philosophy*, provided the original foundation for classical physics, which helps to describe the passage of objects through space.

(a) Isaac Newton's work formed the basis for the laws of physical motion.
(b) Isaac Newton's books on the movement of objects inspired a new understanding of space.

Vocabulary In the context of the passage, ☐ means _____.

1 **features**	(a) highlights	(b) categories	(c) characteristics	(d) manners
2 **radical**	(a) deviant	(b) groundbreaking	(c) fanatical	(d) uncompromising
3 **original**	(a) early	(b) primal	(c) contemporary	(d) preliminary

지문을 읽고 문제에 알맞은 답을 고르세요.

ZURIEL ODUWOLE

Zuriel Oduwole is a female activist best known for promoting the objective of education equality. She has received international recognition for her speeches and films.

Oduwole was born in 2002 in Los Angeles, California, to immigrant parents. Her career started when she produced her first film, *The Ghana Revolution*, at the age of only 10 for a competition at her school.

In 2013, she launched the "Dream Up, Speak Up, Stand Up" campaign, which was aimed at promoting education for girls. As part of the campaign, Oduwole visited schools throughout Africa teaching young girls and their parents about the importance of education.

The following year, at the age of 12, she completed the documentary *A Promising Africa*, which made her the youngest person ever to self-produce a commercial film. In this documentary, Oduwole interviewed some of the most prominent people in Nigeria to showcase the country's recent successes.

While carrying out these activities, Oduwole met one-on-one with many world leaders. They sought her advice on providing opportunities for girls. She has also spoken on issues such as climate change, which was the topic of the talk she delivered to the UN in September 2016.

04 What is Zuriel Oduwole best known for?

(a) advocating girls' education
(b) making speeches in Africa

05 What is included in *A Promising Africa*?

(a) information about female education in Africa
(b) interviews with notable Nigerians

06 Based on the article, why most likely did world leaders meet with Oduwole individually?

(a) They sought her advice about climate change.
(b) They valued her opinion about education.

Vocabulary In the context of the passage, [ ] means _____.

| 4 **objective** | (a) demand | (b) scope | (c) claim | (d) goal |
| 5 **delivered** | (a) brought | (b) gave | (c) planned | (d) accepted |

ALAN MENKEN

Alan Menken is an American composer who achieved fame for his songs in animated movies. Menken is regarded as one of the best composers in contemporary popular music and musical theater.

Menken was born on July 22, 1949, in New York City to Norman and Judith Menken. Norman was a musician, and Judith was an actress. They made sure that Menken took piano and violin lessons as a child. By the age of nine, he had already begun composing his own songs.

After graduating from college, Menken began working with Broadcast Music, Inc. (BMI). BMI's workshops allowed Menken to associate with many people in musical theater, including those from Broadway. This led to his first chance to work as a composer — he was asked to write the music for the musical *God Bless You, Mr. Rosewater*.

Menken's career opportunities ballooned after he began working with Walt Disney Studios. In 1989, Disney hired him to compose songs for *The Little Mermaid*. His song "Under the Sea" won him an Academy Award. He also received Oscars for his work on *Beauty and the Beast*, *Aladdin*, and *Pocahontas*. Currently, Menken holds the record for most Academy Awards among composers alive today, with eight.

07 What did Menken do by the age of nine?

(a) He composed a musical.
(b) He wrote songs of his own.

08 How did working at BMI help Menken's career progress?

(a) by allowing him to connect with people in musical theater
(b) by teaching him how to write successful Broadway musicals

09 Based on the article, what does Menken hold a record in?

(a) He has composed scores for the most Disney movies.
(b) He has more Academy Awards than any other living composer.

Vocabulary In the context of the passage, ☐ means _____.

6	**regarded**	(a) considered	(b) attacked	(c) graded	(d) commemorated
7	**ballooned**	(a) took	(b) steadied	(c) grew	(d) burst

TIGER WOODS

Tiger Woods is an American athlete, who is considered one of the top golfers in history.

Tiger Woods was born on December 30, 1975, in Cypress, California, to Earl and Kultida Woods. His father introduced him to golf before the age of two. His remarkable progress as a young golfer led to instantaneous acclaim, and, by age five, Woods had appeared on television and been featured in *Golf Digest* magazine.

At only eight years of age, Woods won the 1984 Junior World Golf Championships. He became the youngest U.S. Junior Amateur champion in 1991, and won the title again in 1992 and 1993. He remains the only three-time winner of the championship.

After going professional, Woods became the Masters Tournament's youngest winner. He then set the record for being the fastest golfer to reach number one in the world rankings. Woods has also enjoyed tremendous financial success. After his early success, he signed contracts with Nike and Titleist. Though most of his wealth has come through endorsements, Woods has totaled nearly $120 million from tournament wins.

Between 2008 and 2017, Woods's productivity declined due to personal and health issues. However, his career subsequently recovered, and he is winning again.

10 Why most likely was Tiger Woods on television by age five?

(a) because he had knowledge of the history of golf
(b) because he had unusual skill at a young age

11 Which is not one of Tiger Woods's major achievements?

(a) winning the U.S. Junior Amateur championship in successive years
(b) having the most Masters Tournament victories

12 Based on the article, how did Tiger Woods earn most of his wealth?

(a) by making endorsement deals
(b) by winning golf tournaments

정답·해석·해설 p.8

Vocabulary In the context of the passage, ☐ means _____.   Vocabulary 정답·해석 p.11

| 8 **instantaneous** | (a) immediate | (b) prolonged | (c) excessive | (d) gradual |
| 9 **declined** | (a) improved | (b) worsened | (c) rejected | (d) stabilized |

1-7

FERNANDO PESSOA

Fernando Pessoa was a Portuguese writer best known for his extremely wide-ranging literary interests and activities. He is regarded as the most significant Portuguese poet and one of the most notable international literary figures of the early 1900s.

Fernando Pessoa was born on June 13, 1888, in Lisbon, Portugal. He was the son of Joaquim Pessoa and Maria Nogueira. Following his father's death due to tuberculosis, Pessoa moved to South Africa with his mother. There he received an English education, which he later considered to be the foremost factor influencing the course of his life. In high school, he became fluent in English and developed a keen appreciation for English literature, and, in 1903, he won the Queen Victoria Memorial Prize for the best paper in English.

In the following year, a local periodical published one of his poems under the pen name C.R. Anon. Writing under different names became a common practice for Pessoa, who had actually started this habit in childhood when he composed under the name of a fictitious French nobleman, Chevalier de Pas. In total, Pessoa created more than 70 of these imaginary "authors," through which he freely expressed unconventional and controversial viewpoints.

In 1905, Pessoa left his family and returned to Lisbon, where he attempted to study diplomacy. However, he had to give up his studies after two years, in part due to political unrest. Still, his career <u>appeared</u> promising when he inherited enough money from his grandmother to open a publishing company. Unfortunately, this enterprise was ultimately unprofitable and short lived.

For the next two decades, Pessoa moved around continually within Lisbon, renting short-term rooms while surviving on his work as a freelance translator. Meanwhile, he participated in various <u>bold</u> literary projects, increasingly focusing his attention on literary criticism. He and other writers introduced modernist literature to Portuguese magazines such as *Orpheu*, but these efforts were not widely appreciated. Pessoa also avidly studied and wrote about mystical topics like magic and secret societies.

Pessoa died in 1935 at the age of 47, possibly due to alcoholism. In the 1940s, publications of his poetry began to reach a wider audience, and, by the 1980s, he was internationally recognized as an important writer. Some of his work is still unavailable, as over 25,000 pages of his unpublished manuscripts are currently being edited.

1. What is Fernando Pessoa best known for?

   (a) his influence on other Portuguese writers
   (b) promoting English literature in his work
   (c) his ability to compose in a variety of languages
   (d) being interested in different aspects of literature

2. Based on the article, which was the most influential aspect of Pessoa's life?

   (a) the death of his father
   (b) relocating to South Africa
   (c) his schooling in English
   (d) winning an award for best paper

3. Why most likely did he create imaginary authors?

   (a) to include contentious content in his work
   (b) to avoid criticism for the quality of the writing
   (c) because a local periodical required it for publication
   (d) because he encountered it in French literature as a child

4. When did Pessoa work as a freelance translator?

   (a) while studying diplomacy at university
   (b) during his time living in South Africa
   (c) after his publishing company failed
   (d) before his grandmother passed away

5. Why is some of Pessoa's work not available?

   (a) His reputation was ruined by his alcoholism.
   (b) He refused to publish many of his manuscripts.
   (c) Many of his writings are still going through editing.
   (d) Few modern literary critics admire his work.

6. In the context of the passage, <u>appeared</u> means _____.

   (a) occurred
   (b) seemed
   (c) turned
   (d) proved

7. In the context of the passage, <u>bold</u> means _____.

   (a) daring
   (b) strange
   (c) unique
   (d) heroic

SALVADOR DALÍ

Salvador Dalí was a Spanish painter best remembered for his surrealist works. His imagination and unmistakable style, along with his unusual personality, made him one of the most memorable artists of his generation.

Salvador Dalí was born on May 11, 1904, in a town named Figueres, near the Spanish border with France, to a relatively well-off family. His father was a lawyer with no interest in art, and his mother was a homemaker who prompted Dalí to focus on his creative endeavors. When he was 17, he enrolled in the Royal Academy of Fine Arts in Madrid. His work was quickly noticed by his peers due to its use of Cubism, a Parisian avant-garde style that had not yet reached Madrid. His peculiar personality also emerged during this period, as he started to act and dress in an eccentric fashion.

In 1925, Dalí held his first solo art show, and, the following year, he left the Royal Academy prior to completing his studies. He traveled to Paris and met one of his idols, Pablo Picasso. Picasso had already heard of Dalí through Joan Miró, both of whom would profoundly influence Dalí's style. The fantastical elements of this style were clear when he started collaborating with Surrealist artists and filmmakers, such as Luis Buñuel. This group, which celebrated art like Dalí's that explored the world of dreams, invited him to officially join in 1929.

In 1931, Dalí painted his most well-known work, *The Persistence of Memory*, which would become emblematic of Surrealism. This painting represents time's passage through the symbol of a clock that is in process of melting in the heat, suggesting the inevitability of decay. It and other works were featured in Dalí's 1934 exhibit in New York, where his paintings and his personality created a sensation among art enthusiasts. Dalí produced many other iconic works throughout the rest of the decade, including the *Lobster Telephone* and *Soft Construction with Boiled Beans (Premonition of Civil War)*, one of the few political paintings he completed.

Dalí's later works were not as highly regarded as his previous creations, and he spent much of the last few decades of his life designing the Dalí Theatre and Museum to display his paintings in his hometown. After a decade of poor health, Dalí died of heart failure in 1989.

8. Which is true about Salvador Dalí's childhood?

   (a) His family was originally from France.
   (b) His father was opposed to his artistic interests.
   (c) His mother was once an artist.
   (d) His parents were reasonably wealthy.

9. What did Dalí start to do during his studies in the Royal Academy of Fine Arts?

   (a) paint in a surrealist style
   (b) dress in unusual clothes
   (c) act in avant-garde plays
   (d) imitate his peer's Cubist works

10. Based on the article, why most likely was he invited to become a Surrealist?

   (a) because of the dream-like style of his paintings
   (b) because he was friends with Luis Buñuel
   (c) because of the surrealism of The Persistence of Memory
   (d) because he had met Pablo Picasso

11. What does The Persistence of Memory represent?

   (a) It represents the decay of the art world.
   (b) It represents the political chaos of the civil war.
   (c) It represents the sensational persona of Dalí.
   (d) It represents the way that time moves forward.

12. How did Dalí spend the last few decades of his life?

   (a) constructing a theater and museum in Paris
   (b) creating an institution for his works
   (c) working on political artworks
   (d) painting his most celebrated works

13. In the context of the passage, prompted means _____.

   (a) goaded
   (b) forced
   (c) irritated
   (d) motivated

14. In the context of the passage, previous means _____.

   (a) primary
   (b) preliminary
   (c) foremost
   (d) earlier

LE CORBUSIER

Le Corbusier was a Swiss architect notable for his opposition to tradition. His modernist architecture is featured in numerous countries across the globe.

Le Corbusier was born on October 6, 1887, in a French-speaking town in Switzerland, where his father was an artisan and his mother was a piano teacher. He became interested in art during his teenage years, and he enrolled in a school founded by the painter Charles L'Eplattenier. Despite preferring other forms of art, Le Corbusier was instructed to study architecture by L'Eplattenier, and he chose not to <u>defy</u> this order.

Le Corbusier's first jobs after graduating were designing homes, mostly in the local style of mountain houses. A trip to Italy in 1907 opened his eyes to the world outside of his country for the first time. He was particularly impressed with the practical design of the Florence Charterhouse, a northern Italian monastery. Le Corbusier viewed its efficient division into many individual cells as a potential solution to the need for urban apartment housing.

In 1917, Le Corbusier moved to Paris and started his own architectural firm. His first significant commission was a pavilion for the 1925 International Exhibition of Modern Decorative and Industrial Arts. Le Corbusier's pavilion embodied his <u>practice</u> of creating open spaces without decoration. It was ridiculed by critics for its lack of walls, and some even tried to hide its exposed interior from spectators. However, there were others who admired its modern style and commissioned Le Corbusier to build houses for them because of it. Many of these structures are now considered classics of modern architecture, such as the Villa Savoye.

Over the next decades, Le Corbusier designed a range of buildings throughout Europe and America for both rich clients and municipal governments. He struggled to find work following the outbreak of World War II, but after the war ended, he was able to complete the Unité d'habitation in Marseille, which some considered his greatest achievement. This apartment complex reflected Le Corbusier's democratic ideas about architecture and is recognized as one of the most influential designs of all time.

Le Corbusier ultimately planned entire communities and cities during his life. He also painted, co-founded the Purist art movement, and wrote extensively about architecture. He died abruptly in 1965 during a swim in the Mediterranean Sea, presumably from a heart attack.

15. What is Le Corbusier known for?

    (a) being opposed to convention
    (b) his work at a famous architectural school
    (c) designing pavilions around the world
    (d) his interest in art in his youth

16. What led Le Corbusier to study architecture?

    (a) his parents' insistence
    (b) his love of art and design
    (c) his teacher's command
    (d) his ambition to be an architect

17. Based on the article, why was he impressed by the Florence Charterhouse?

    (a) because it showed how to reduce urban housing costs
    (b) because it made efficient use of space
    (c) because it was naturally situated in the mountains
    (d) because it had an elaborate but utilitarian design

18. Why most likely was Le Corbusier's pavilion criticized?

    (a) because it was too decorative
    (b) because it could not be seen by spectators
    (c) because it was considered too open
    (d) because it was not thought to be modern

19. Where did Le Corbusier build the Unité d'habitation?

    (a) in Florence
    (b) in Switzerland
    (c) in Paris
    (d) in Marseille

20. In the context of the passage, defy means _____.

    (a) follow
    (b) disobey
    (c) consider
    (d) hate

21. In the context of the passage, practice means _____.

    (a) policy
    (b) trait
    (c) formula
    (d) method

HOMER J. SIMPSON

Homer J. Simpson is a fictional character on the American animated sitcom *The Simpsons*, a show originally created as a two-minute short by cartoonist Matt Groening for *The Tracey Ullman Show* in 1987. It was bought by the Fox Network in 1989 and turned into a successful weekly half-hour program in the network's prime-time lineup. The show parodies American culture and society through the lives of its namesake family and a collection of other characters inhabiting the town of Springfield.

Physically, Homer is balding and overweight with distinctive hair and stubble that instantaneously reappears after shaving. He is typically dressed in a white shirt with short sleeves, blue pants, and gray shoes. He is married to Marge and has three young children, Bart, Lisa, and Maggie. He utters the trademark expression "D'oh!" whenever he injures himself, realizes his stupidity, or has otherwise had some unfortunate fate befall him. His foolish and impulsive behavior is regularly exploited for comic effect.

Matt Groening named Homer after his father but has emphasized that they are otherwise completely dissimilar. The middle initial "J" stands for "Jay", and is a tribute to the characters Bullwinkle J. Moose and Rocket J. Squirrel from the iconic 1960s cartoon program, *The Rocky and Bullwinkle Show*, themselves named after creator Jay Ward. From the beginning, Homer has been voiced by Dan Castellaneta, who was a cast member on the *Tracey Ullman Show* and who does other characters on *The Simpsons*.

In the show, Homer is normally employed as a nuclear safety inspector at the Springfield Nuclear Power Plant, a job for which he is supremely unqualified and makes the least effort possible. He is portrayed as a dumb and immature everyman who is otherwise loyal and protective of his family. At the same time, he embodies the stereotypical qualities of American blue-collar types: hopelessly unsophisticated, aggressively outspoken, and addicted to beer, junk food, and television. Whereas other characters on *The Simpsons* might have counterparts in other cultures, Homer is, as author Chris Turner describes him, "pure American".

All told, Homer's appeal and popularity have endured for over two decades. He has been a subject of scrutiny for cultural scholars and social scientists and become a mainstay of American television. His likeness can be found plastered on a wide variety of merchandise along with other characters from the show.

22. What happened after *The Simpsons* was acquired by the Fox Network?

   (a) New characters were introduced.
   (b) It was given a longer running time.
   (c) Homer was voiced by a different actor.
   (d) It was moved to a daytime schedule.

23. According to the article, when does Homer use his trademark expression?

   (a) when he wants to emphasize a point
   (b) when he feels annoyed by his children
   (c) when he is victimized by bad luck
   (d) when he successfully plays a prank

24. Where does Homer's middle initial come from?

   (a) a biological relative of his creator
   (b) a cartoon from the 1960s
   (c) a cartoonist who served as a mentor
   (d) a collaborator on the program

25. Which is NOT a quality that describes Homer?

   (a) intellectually inferior
   (b) devoted to his family
   (c) emotionally underdeveloped
   (d) committed to his profession

26. What does Chris Turner probably mean by his characterization of Homer?

   (a) Homer's laid-back nature makes him an easy character to relate to.
   (b) Homer provides a good representation of American values to other cultures.
   (c) Homer's popularity has been used to great advantage for commercial profit.
   (d) Homer displays the traits that are commonly associated with typical Americans.

27. In the context of the passage, exploited means _____.

   (a) berated
   (b) mistreated
   (c) manipulated
   (d) disciplined

28. In the context of the passage, supremely means _____.

   (a) extremely
   (b) excellently
   (c) flawlessly
   (d) wonderfully

2주 만에 끝내는 해커스 지텔프 독해 Level 2

JEFF GORDON

Jeff Gordon is an American former stock-car racing driver, who is best known for winning four NASCAR Cup Series championships in seven seasons. He is credited with boosting the popularity of NASCAR racing among American audiences.

Born in Vallejo, California, on August 4, 1971, Gordon is the son of Carol Ann Bickford and William Grinnell Gordon, who divorced when he was less than a year old. His stepfather, whom his mother married in the mid-70s, gave him a BMX bike when he was four, which sparked his love of racing. A year later, he started racing quarter midget cars and by the time he was six, he had already won 35 races, setting five speed records on different tracks along the way.

He continued to race throughout his childhood and adolescence, and at 16, was the youngest driver ever to receive a United States Auto Club license. His success as a midget-car racer brought him to the attention of restaurateur Hugh Connerty, who provided the sponsorship for Gordon to make his debut as a stock-car racer in the NASCAR Busch Grand National, a minor league circuit for younger drivers.

In 1991, Gordon joined Bill Davis's team as full-time driver in the Busch Grand National. He was an immediate success, setting a new record with 11 poles in a season and winning the Rookie of the Year award. The following year, he joined the Cup Series, the main NASCAR series, where he again won Rookie of the Year.

The early years of Gordon's NASCAR career were characterized by a number of dangerous crashes, thanks to his aggressive driving style. Many NASCAR commentators therefore doubted Gordon could compete for the championship. Gordon disregarded these opinions and in 1994 won the championship with a lead of 300 points over his nearest rival. He followed this up with a second-place finish in 1996 and back-to-back championships in 1997 and 1998.

Gordon went on to secure one more championship before finally retiring from full-time driving in 2015, although he has competed sparingly as a substitute driver since then. He ended his career with 93 race victories, which placed him third in the all-time ranking of NASCAR drivers. He currently works as an executive for the Hendrick Motorsports racing team and as a television announcer for NASCAR races.

29. What is Jeff Gordon best known for?

   (a) earning the most championship
       victories in NASCAR history
   (b) building a successful NASCAR racing
       team
   (c) getting Rookie of the Year awards in
       two successive seasons
   (d) winning four seasons of NASCAR
       racing

30. Which is true of Gordon's childhood?

   (a) His parents were divorced before he
       was born.
   (b) His stepfather gave him his first racing
       car.
   (c) He broke the speed record on several
       courses.
   (d) He started racing midget cars when he
       was six.

31. When did Gordon's career as a NASCAR
    racer start?

   (a) after he received his first Rookie of the
       Year award
   (b) during his time riding BMX bikes
   (c) before he got his United States Auto
       Club license
   (d) when he was sponsored by Hugh
       Connerty

32. What is most likely the reason NASCAR
    commentators doubted Gordon's ability?

   (a) Gordon's style of racing often led to
       accidents.
   (b) Gordon's car was not fast enough to
       beat his rivals.
   (c) Gordon was thought to have an
       aggressive personality.
   (d) Gordon was considered too young to
       win the championship.

33. What did Gordon do after retiring from
    full-time racing?

   (a) became a chief executive in a
       company
   (b) became a reporter for a TV show
   (c) became a racing team director
   (d) became a manager of a channel

34. In the context of the passage, disregarded
    means _____.

   (a) noticed
   (b) neglected
   (c) mistreated
   (d) ignored

35. In the context of the passage, sparingly
    means _____.

   (a) usually
   (b) infrequently
   (c) mostly
   (d) randomly

정답·해석·해설 p.11

PART 1에서 선별한 다음의 지텔프 빈출 어휘들을 암기한 후 퀴즈로 확인해보세요.

renown n. 명성	**recent** adj. 최근의, 근대의
appearance n. 출연, 겉모습	**success** n. 성공한 사람, 성과
performance n. 연기, 공연	**advocate** v. 고취하다, 지지하다
decade n. 10년	**individually** adv. 개인적으로, 따로따로
humble adj. 허름한, 초라한	**value** v. 높이 평가하다, 소중하게 여기다
international adj. 국제적인	**composer** n. 작곡가
radical adj. 혁신적인, 급진적인	**achieve** v. 얻다
limit v. 막다, 제한하다	**fame** n. 명성, 인기
distribute v. 배포하다, 나누어주다	**allow** v. ~할 수 있게 하다
affordable adj. 저렴한, (가격이) 알맞은	**athlete** n. 운동선수
devise v. 창시하다, 고안하다	**remarkable** adj. 우수한
classical adj. 고전의	**acclaim** n. 찬사
activist n. 운동가	**wealth** n. 재산
immigrant adj. 이민자의	**tournament** n. 대회
competition n. 대회, 경쟁	**subsequently** adv. 그 후에
importance n. 중요성	**knowledge** n. 지식
prominent adj. 유명한	**figure** n. 인물, 숫자

Quiz 각 단어의 알맞은 뜻을 찾아 연결하세요.

01 decade	ⓐ 고취하다, 지지하다	06 immigrant	ⓗ 인물, 숫자
02 renown	ⓑ 유명한	07 classical	ⓘ 우수한
03 acclaim	ⓒ 찬사	08 remarkable	ⓙ 운동가
04 advocate	ⓓ 명성	09 activist	ⓚ 고전의
05 prominent	ⓔ 얻다	10 subsequently	ⓛ 국제적인
	ⓕ 10년		ⓜ 이민자의
	ⓖ 지식		ⓝ 그 후에

ⓝ 01 ⓓ 02 ⓒ 03 ⓐ 04 ⓑ 05 ⓜ 06 ⓚ 07 ⓘ 08 ⓙ 09 ⓝ 10 정답

course n. 진로, 과정

controversial adj. 논쟁의 여지가 있는

enterprise n. 기업, 회사

criticism n. 비평, 평론

alcoholism n. 알코올 중독

ability n. 능력

encounter v. 접하다, 마주하다

pass away phr. 돌아가시다, 사망하다

admire v. 칭찬하다, 존경하다

memorable adj. 인상적인, 기억할 만한

relatively adv. 상대적으로

prompt v. 고무하다, 부추기다

endeavor n. 시도, 노력

enroll v. 입학하다, 등록하다

peculiar adj. 독특한

collaborate v. 함께 작업하다

celebrate v. 찬양하다, 칭찬하다

display v. 전시하다

oppose v. 반대하다

imitate v. 모방하다, 따라 하다

institution n. 시설, 기관

potential adj. 잠재적인

ambition n. 야망

instantaneously adv. 즉시, 순간적으로

exploit v. 이용하다

unqualified adj. 자격이 없는

merchandise n. 상품

boost v. 끌어올리다, 후원하다

divorce v. 이혼하다

adolescence n. 청소년기

sponsorship n. 후원

aggressive adj. 공격적인

doubt v. 믿지 않다, 의심하다

executive n. 임원, 관리직

Quiz 각 단어의 알맞은 뜻을 찾아 연결하세요.

01 ambition	ⓐ 이혼하다	06 enroll	ⓗ 기업, 회사
02 prompt	ⓑ 독특한	07 potential	ⓘ 청소년기
03 divorce	ⓒ 시도, 노력	08 enterprise	ⓙ 입학하다, 등록하다
04 endeavor	ⓓ 고무하다, 부추기다	09 adolescence	ⓚ 진로, 과정
05 controversial	ⓔ 야망	10 criticism	ⓛ 상대적으로
	ⓕ 능력		ⓜ 비평, 평론
	ⓖ 논쟁의 여지가 있는		ⓝ 잠재적인

정답 01 ⓔ 02 ⓓ 03 ⓐ 04 ⓒ 05 ⓖ 06 ⓙ 07 ⓝ 08 ⓗ 09 ⓘ 10 ⓜ

PART

2

잡지/인터넷 기사

Magazine/Web Article

잡지/인터넷 기사 Magazine/Web Article

PART 2에서는 사회적 이슈에 관한 잡지/인터넷 기사 지문이 출제된다. 4개 파트 중에서 유일하게 제목이 문제 풀이의 단서가 되는 지문 유형이며, 지문의 주제와 지문에서 언급된 연구 결과에 대한 세부내용을 묻는 문제가 출제된다.

출제 토픽

최근의 사회적 변화나 과학적 발견 등이 주로 출제된다. 기존에는 고고학, 의학, 건강 관련 연구 결과가 많이 출제되는 편이었으나, 최근에는 사회적 관심거리나 새로운 기술, 제품의 소개를 다루는 지문도 많이 출제되고 있다.

· 사회적 변화	출산율 저하, 밀레니얼 세대의 여행 문화, 2030 세대의 오춘기
· 과학적 발견	탈모 치료 가능성, 좌뇌와 우뇌의 기능, 새로운 유형의 오로라, 고대 도시 발견
· 새로운 기술	자외선 차단 콘택트렌즈, 먹는 숟가락, 먹을 수 있는 물병 '오호'
· 소식/대중문화	'selfie' 옥스퍼드 사전 등재, 'Bless you'의 어원, 비디오 게임

문제 유형

기사의 주제를 묻는 문제나 연구를 통해 알아낸 것, 발견하게 된 것을 묻는 문제가 주로 첫 문제로 출제된다. 목적 문제는 출제되지 않는다.

주제	기사의 주제를 묻는다. **What is the main topic of the article?** 기사의 주제는 무엇인가?
특정세부사항	무엇을, 언제, 어디서, 어떻게 발견한 것인지 등 지문에서 언급된 세부사항을 묻는다. **What** is the effect of humidity on children's eyes? 어린이의 눈에 미치는 습도의 영향은 무엇인가?
Not/True	연구 결과나 제품에 대해 언급된 사건, 업적 등에 대해 사실이거나 사실이 아닌 것을 묻는다. Which of the following is **not true** about igloos? 다음 중 이글루에 관해 사실이 아닌 것은?
추론	연구의 한계나 추후 과제, 연구의 세부내용 등에 대해 추론할 수 있는 것을 묻는다. What is **most likely** the limitation of the experiment? 실험의 한계는 무엇인 것 같은가?
어휘	지문의 문맥에서 밑줄 어휘의 유의어가 무엇인지를 묻는다. In the context of the passage, previous means _____. 지문의 문맥에서, 'previous'는 ~을 의미한다.

핵심 전략

1. '연구 결과 소개 → 연구 계기 → 특징 → 의의/추후 과제'의 패턴화된 흐름에서 출제되는 빈출 문제들을 알아두어야 한다.

2. 연구 결과, 차이점, 시사점을 설명하는 내용은 관련 표현을 익혀두면 쉽게 찾을 수 있다.

3. 지문의 제목에서 주로 주제가 드러나므로, 제목을 확인해두면 지문의 전반적인 내용을 이해할 때 도움이 된다.

스티로폼을 대체할 새로운
섬유질 단열재를 공개하다

워싱턴 주립대학교 연구원들이 스티로폼을
대체할 수 있는 단열재를 개발하는 데에 성
공했다. 이것은 식물 섬유질로 만들어졌고,
물을 사용해서 쉽게 제조할 수 있다는 것이
특징이다. 이 연구 성과는 영국에서 발행하
는 바이오 소재 전문 학술지 「카보하이드레
이트 폴리머스」에 게재되었다.

워싱턴 주립대학교의 부교수인 아메르 아멜
리와 샤오 장은 스티로폼을 대체할 친환경
소재를 개발했다고 발표했다. 이 연구는 여
러 장점으로 인해 널리 이용되고 있지만, 유
독성 물질로 만들어져서 환경 오염에 큰 영
향을 끼치고 있는 스티로폼을 대체할 단열
재를 개발하기 위해 진행되었다.

연구팀은 75퍼센트 섬유질에 폴리비닐 알
코올을 더하였는데, 이는 균등한 세포 구조
를 통해 탁월한 단열 기능을 가진다. 이전
것들은 단열 기능이 떨어질 뿐만 아니라, 잘
부서지고, 고온 다습한 환경에서 쉽게 분해
되었는데, 이 단점을 보완하면서 스티로폼
만큼 성능이 좋은 것을 개발한 것은 이번이
처음이다.

이번 연구 결과는 재생 가능한 신소재의 추
가 발전 가능성을 보여주기 때문에 큰 의의
가 있다. 장 교수는 "이 섬유질 단열재는 많
은 잠재력을 가지고 있고, 이를 더 발전시킬
생각에 설렙니다."라고 말했다.

연구원들은 이 소재의 내구성을 높이는 방
법과 더 저렴한 비용으로 생산할 방법을 추
가로 연구하는 중이다. 이를 통해 스티로폼
을 대신하는 친환경적인 단열재가 상품화될
수 있도록 하는 것이 그들의 최종 목표이다.

지문 흐름

흐름에 따른 빈출 문제

연구 결과 소개

지문의 주제를 묻는 문제가 주로 출제된다.
ex What is the topic of the article?
기사의 주제는 무엇인가?

연구를 통해 알아낸 것을 묻는 문제가 주로 출제된다.
ex What did the study find out?
연구는 무엇을 알아냈는가?

연구의 계기

관련된 인물 및 회사에 관해 묻는 문제가 출제된다.
ex Why did the WSU research team conduct the research?
워싱턴 주립대학교 연구팀은 왜 이 연구를 시행했는가?

연구의 계기가 된 문제점을 묻는 문제가 출제된다.
ex What is the problem with Styrofoam?
스티로폼의 문제점은 무엇인가?

연구 결과의 특징

어떻게 개발 · 발견했는지를 묻는 문제가 출제된다.
ex How did the research team develop the environmentally friendly insulator?
연구팀은 어떻게 친환경 단열재를 개발했는가?

이전 연구 결과와의 차이를 묻는 문제가 출제된다.
ex What is the difference between previous materials and the newly developed material?
이전 물질과 새롭게 개발된 물질의 차이는 무엇인가?

연구의 의의 및 시사점

연구의 의의나 시사점을 묻는 문제가 출제된다.
ex What are the researchers most likely suggesting about the new insulator?
연구원들이 새로운 단열재에 대해 무엇을 시사하는 것 같은가?

추후 과제

연구의 추후 과제를 묻는 문제가 출제된다.
ex What are scientists now researching to achieve their goal?
연구원들은 이제 그들의 목표를 성취하기 위해 무엇을 연구하고 있는가?

1. 주제 및 연구 결과

① **A study shows that**   연구는 ~을 보여준다

A study shows that the microbes causing Parkinson's may originate in the gut.

연구는 파킨슨병을 유발하는 미생물이 내장에서 생길 수도 있음을 보여준다.

② 연구/사람 **discovered/found**   (연구/사람)이 ~을 발견했다/알아냈다

A team of researchers has **discovered** a new type of star.

연구팀이 새로운 유형의 항성을 발견했다.

③ 사람/기관 **launched/announced**   (사람/기관)이 ~을 개시했다/발표했다

Eliot Wright, the founder of Multipass, recently **launched** the company's newest venture.

멀티패스 사의 설립자인 엘리엇 라이트는 최근에 회사의 새로운 사업을 개시했다.

2. 차이점

④ **The difference is**   차이는 ~이다

The most noticeable **difference is** how much bigger the irises are in the male.

가장 눈에 띄는 차이는 수컷의 홍채 크기가 얼마나 더 크냐는 것이다.

⑤ **A is** 비교급 **than B**   A가 B보다 ~하다

Mars **is** much **colder than** Earth, as it is farther from the sun.

화성은 태양에서 더 멀기 때문에 지구보다 훨씬 더 기온이 낮다.

3. 시사점

⑥ **The discovery suggests that**   발견은 ~을 시사한다

The discovery suggests that interactions between humans and Neanderthals were common.

발견은 인간과 네안데르탈인들 간의 상호 작용이 흔했다는 것을 시사한다.

⑦ **The studies shed light on**   연구는 ~을 설명한다

The studies shed light on the way that physical exercise improves cognitive functions.

연구는 신체 운동이 인지 기능을 향상시키는 방법을 설명한다.

1. 연구 결과 및 발견

identify v. 확인하다, 발견하다

state v. 말하다, 서술하다

indicate v. 나타내다, 보여주다

conclude v. 결론을 내리다

result n. 결과 v. 발생하다, 기인하다

proof n. 증거

2. 연구 계기 및 과정

record n. 기록 v. 기록하다

device n. 장치, 기기

specimen n. 견본, 샘플

participant n. 참가자

subject n. 연구 대상, 주제

compare v. 비교하다, 필적하다

analyze v. 분석하다

observe v. 관찰하다, 보다

conduct v. 수행하다, 처리하다

experiment n. 실험

examine v. 조사하다, 검사하다

determine v. 알아내다, 밝히다

aim v. 목표하다 n. 목표

enhance v. 향상시키다

3. 특징 및 세부사항

prehistoric adj. 선사 시대의

extinct adj. 멸종된

alternative n. 대안, 대체 adj. 대안이 되는

constant adj. 변함없는, 끊임없는

artificial adj. 인공의

significant adj. 중요한, 커다란

similar adj. 비슷한

different adj. 다른

typical adj. 전형적인, 대표적인

moderate adj. 보통의, 중간의

severe adj. 극심한, 혹독한

frequent adj. 잦은, 빈번한

4. 한계 및 과제

limitation n. 한계, 제약

challenge n. 과제, 난제, 도전

argue v. 주장하다, 다투다

potential adj. 잠재적인, 가능성이 있는

advantage n. 이점, 장점

support v. 지지하다, 뒷받침하다

RESEARCHERS DISCOVER NEW SPECIES OF CLAM IN OCEAN'S DEPTHS

1번 키워드

1   In a paper in the Journal of Molluscan Studies, **zoologists at Chicago's Field Museum have announced the discovery of a new species of wood-boring clam living in the deep oceans**. The animal had previously been observed but has only now been classified, identifying it as a member of the Mollusca family.

연구 결과
소개

2   The new species is called gilsonorum in honor of the Gilsons, longtime supporters of the Field Museum. Like other wood-boring clams, the gilsonorum digs into wood with its shell and consumes what it scrapes off, **using bacteria in its gills to help it digest the material**.

2번 키워드

연구 대상의
특징

3   The finding is significant because it shows that wood-boring clams are more diverse than initially thought. Scientists have previously struggled to categorize the clams, as variations between them are hard to detect based on appearance alone. They also live deep underwater and **must be retrieved by robot submersibles and transported to a lab on land for examination**. The existence of this separate gilsonorum species of wood-boring clam was only confirmed after DNA tests.

3번 키워드

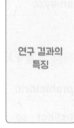
연구 결과의
특징

4   Wood-boring clams are important creatures to study as they are crucial to the ecosystem. Though often no more than a centimeter long, they converge in such large numbers that they impact the environment in significant ways. Most importantly, **they convert carbon into a form that other animals can eat**.

4번 키워드

연구의 의의
및 시사점

5   Scientists speculate that these clams play a vital role in cleaning up the millions of tons of wood on the ocean floor, which would otherwise rot. **By removing such a large quantity of wood, they may even be able to affect sea level rise**, although this hypothesis has yet to be tested.

5번 키워드

추후 과제

주제를 묻고 있으므로, 연구 결과를 소개하는
제목 및 1단락에서 단서를 찾는다.

1. What is the main topic of the magazine
   article?

   (a) the life-cycle of the wood-boring clam

   (b) the environmental impact of clams

   (c) the finding of a clam that drills into wood

   (d) the discovery of a clam that consumes
       trash

소화를 돕는 것이 무엇인지를 묻고 있으므
로, 질문의 키워드 helps ~ digestion이
help it digest로 paraphrasing되어 언
급된 2단락에서 단서를 찾는다.

2. What helps the clams' digestion?

   (a) special muscles in their shells

   (b) bacteria in their gills

   (c) their wood-boring teeth

   (d) the underwater pressure

어떻게 연구했는지를 묻고 있으므로, 질문의 키
워드 examine이 examination으로 언급된
3단락에서 단서를 찾는다.

3. How did the researchers examine the clams?

   (a) by transporting them to solid ground

   (b) by diving down in submarine vehicles

   (c) by using a robot in a laboratory

   (d) by investigating the creatures' ocean
       habitats

환경에 도움이 되는 방식에 대해 사실인 것을 묻고
있으므로, 질문의 키워드 environment가 그대
로 언급된 4단락에서 단서를 찾는다.

4. Which is true about the way wood-boring clams
   help the environment?

   (a) They maintain the plant life in the deep
       ocean.

   (b) They clean up after other sea creatures.

   (c) They generate carbon dioxide in the
       oceans.

   (d) They make a substance edible for fish.

어떻게 해수면에 영향을 미칠 수 있을 것 같은지를 묻고
있으므로, 질문의 키워드 sea levels가 sea level로
언급된 5단락에서 단서를 찾는다.

5. According to the passage, how most likely could
   wood-boring clams affect sea levels?

   (a) by disposing of their shells after they die

   (b) by decomposing wood to release carbon

   (c) by cleaning up excess plastic waste
       dumped in the ocean

   (d) by clearing a large amount of wood from
       the sea

6. In the context of the passage, identifying means
   _____.

   (a) calling

   (b) selecting

   (c) recognizing

   (d) involving

7. In the context of the passage, variations means
   _____.

   (a) innovations

   (b) differences

   (c) similarities

   (d) fluctuations

해석 및 해설 뒷장에서 확인하기 ➡

PART 2

2주 막힘 없는 해커스 지털프 독해 Level 2

연구자들이 바다 깊은 곳에서 새로운 조개류를 발견하다

1 연체동물 연구 학술지의 한 논문에서, [1]시카고 필드 박물관의 동물학자들이 심해에 사는 목질부에 구멍을 뚫는 새로운 조개류의 발견을 발표했다. 그 동물은 이전에 관측되었으나 이제서야 분류되어, 그것이 연체동물과의 일원임을 <u>식별했다</u>.

2 이 새로운 종은 필드 박물관의 오랜 후원자인 Gilson 가를 기리기 위해 gilsonorum으로 불린다. 목질부에 구멍을 뚫는 다른 조개들처럼, gilsonorum은 그것의 껍데기로 나무를 파헤쳐 벗겨낸 것을 섭취하는데, [2]이때 그 물질을 소화하도록 돕기 위해 아가미 안에 있는 박테리아를 이용한다.

3 이 발견은 중요한데 그것이 목질부에 구멍을 뚫는 조개가 처음에 생각된 것보다 더 다양하다는 것을 보여주기 때문이다. 과학자들은 이전에 그 조개들을 분류하는 데 어려움을 겪어왔는데, 이는 생김새에만 근거해서는 그것들 간의 <u>차이</u>를 알아내기 어렵기 때문이다. 그것들은 또한 깊은 물속에 살며 [3]잠수정 로봇에 의해 회수되어 조사를 위해 육지의 실험실로 옮겨져야 한다. 이 구분된 목질부에 구멍을 뚫는 조개류 gilsonorum의 존재는 DNA 검사 이후에야 입증되었다.

4 목질부에 구멍을 뚫는 조개는 연구하기에 중요한 생물체인데 그것이 생태계에 있어 중대하기 때문이다. 대개 1센티미터가 안 되는 길이에 불과하지만, 그것들은 매우 많은 수가 한곳에 모이기 때문에 중요한 방식으로 환경에 영향을 미친다. 가장 중요하게도, [4]그것들은 탄소를 다른 동물들이 섭취할 수 있는 형태로 전환한다.

5 과학자들은 이러한 조개들이 해저에 있는 수백만 톤의 목재를 청소하는 데 중요한 역할을 할 것이라고 상정하는데, 그렇지 않으면 그것은 썩을 것이었다. 비록 이 가설은 아직 확인되지 않았지만, [5]그렇게 엄청난 양의 목재를 제거함으로써, 그것들은 심지어 해수면 상승에도 영향을 미칠 수 있을지도 모른다.

어휘 **clam** n. 조개 **journal** n. 학술지 **molluscan** n. 연체동물 **zoologist** n. 동물학자 **wood-boring** adj. 목질부에 구멍을 뚫는
previously adv. 이전에 **observe** v. 관측하다 **classify** v. 분류하다 **identify** v. 식별하다, 확인하다
in honor of phr. ~을 기리기 위해, 기념하여 **dig into** phr. ~을 파헤치다 **consume** v. 섭취하다 **scrape off** phr. 벗겨내다
gill n. 아가미 **digest** v. 소화하다 **significant** adj. 중요한 **diverse** adj. 다양한 **initially** adv. 처음에, 초기에
struggle v. 어려움을 겪다, 분투하다 **categorize** v. 분류하다 **variation** n. 차이, 다양성 **detect** v. 알아내다, 감지하다
appearance n. 생김새 **retrieve** v. 회수하다, 탐색하다 **submersible** n. 잠수정 **transport** v. 옮기다 **examination** n. 조사, 검토
existence n. 존재 **separate** adj. 구분된, 별개의 **confirm** v. 입증하다 **ecosystem** n. 생태계 **converge** v. (한 곳에) 모이다
convert v. 전환하다 **speculate** v. 상정하다 **rot** v. 썩다, 부패하다 **sea level** phr. 해수면 **hypothesis** n. 가설

1. 주제/목적 기사의 주제　　　　　　　정답 (c)

해석 잡지 기사의 주제는 무엇인가?
(a) 목질부에 구멍을 뚫는 조개의 생활 주기
(b) 조개의 환경적인 영향
(c) 나무에 구멍을 뚫는 조개의 발견
(d) 쓰레기를 섭취하는 조개의 발견

해설 1단락의 'zoologists ~ have announced the discovery of a new species of wood-boring clam living in the deep oceans'에서 동물학자들이 심해에 사는 목질부에 구멍을 뚫는 새로운 조개류의 발견을 발표했다고 한 뒤, 나무에 구멍을 뚫는 조개의 발견에 관한 내용이 이어지고 있다. 따라서 (c)가 정답이다.

2. 특정세부사항 What　　　　　　　정답 (b)

해석 조개의 소화를 돕는 것은 무엇인가?
(a) 껍데기 안에 있는 특별한 근육
(b) 아가미 안에 있는 박테리아
(c) 목질부에 구멍을 뚫는 이빨
(d) 물속의 압력

해설 2단락의 'using bacteria in its gills to help it digest the material'에서 물질을 소화하도록 돕기 위해 아가미 안에 있는 박테리아를 이용한다고 했다. 따라서 (b)가 정답이다.

3. 특정세부사항 How　　　　　　　정답 (a)

해석 연구원들은 어떻게 조개를 연구했는가?
(a) 그것들을 지면으로 옮김으로써
(b) 잠수함으로 물속에 들어감으로써
(c) 연구실에서 로봇을 사용함으로써
(d) 그 생물체의 바다 서식지를 연구함으로써

해설 3단락의 'must be retrieved by robot submersibles and transported to a lab on land for examination'에서 잠수정 로봇에 의해 회수되어 조사를 위해 육지의 실험실로 옮겨져야 한다고 했다. 따라서 (a)가 정답이다.

4. Not/True True 문제　　　　　　　정답 (d)

해석 목질부에 구멍을 뚫는 조개가 환경에 도움이 되는 방식에 대해 사실인 것은?
(a) 심해의 식물을 보존시킨다.
(b) 다른 해양 생물체의 뒤를 깨끗이 청소한다.
(c) 바다에서 이산화탄소를 내뱉는다.
(d) 물질을 물고기가 섭취할 수 있게 만든다.

해설 4단락의 'they convert carbon into a form that other animals can eat'에서 조개는 탄소를 다른 동물들이 섭취할 수 있는 형태로 전환한다고 했다. 따라서 (d)가 정답이다.

5. 추론 특정사실　　　　　　　정답 (d)

해석 지문에 따르면, 목질부에 구멍을 뚫는 조개는 어떻게 해수면에 영향을 미칠 수 있을 것 같은가?
(a) 죽은 다음에 껍데기를 없앰으로써
(b) 목재가 탄소를 방출하도록 분해함으로써
(c) 바다에 버려진 과잉 플라스틱 폐기물을 치움으로써
(d) 바다의 많은 목재를 없앰으로써

해설 5단락의 'By removing such a large quantity of wood, they may even be able to affect sea level rise'에서 엄청난 양의 목재를 제거함으로써 심지어 해수면 상승에도 영향을 미칠 수 있을지도 모른다고 했다. 따라서 (d)가 정답이다.

6. 어휘 유의어　　　　　　　정답 (c)

해석 지문의 문맥에서, 'identifying'은 -을 의미한다.
(a) 부르다
(b) 선택하다
(c) 인식하다
(d) 포함하다

해설 1단락의 'identifying it as a member of the Mollusca family'는 그 동물이 연체동물과의 일원임을 '식별했다'는 뜻이므로, '인식하다'라는 비슷한 의미의 (c)가 정답이다.

7. 어휘 유의어　　　　　　　정답 (b)

해석 지문의 문맥에서, 'variations'는 -을 의미한다.
(a) 혁신
(b) 차이
(c) 유사성
(d) 변동

해설 3단락의 'variations between them are hard to detect based on appearance alone'은 생김새에만 근거해서는 조개들 간의 '차이'를 알아내기 어렵다는 뜻이므로, '차이'라는 같은 의미의 (b)가 정답이다.

지문의 내용을 올바르게 paraphrasing한 것을 고르세요.

01

> Paleontologists have discovered an unprecedented collection of fossilized remains that could help explain how the dinosaurs died. However, the finding has drawn skepticism after a magazine report on it differed significantly from scientific reports.

(a) The differences between a magazine article and scientific reports led to doubt.
(b) A popular science magazine gave an inaccurate report on how the dinosaurs died.

02

> New York's Central Park has erected its first statues of female historical figures. Cast in bronze by artist Meredith Bergman, the two figures are Susan B. Anthony and Elizabeth C. Stanton, who fought for women's voting rights.

(a) A famous sculpture that was the first to be produced by two women was installed in Central Park.
(b) Sculptures depicting historical women were put up in Central Park for the first time.

03

> Researchers have detected over 400 bacteria specimens living on the surfaces of microplastics, which are tiny plastic pieces of discarded products that accumulate in oceans. Some of these bacteria are harmful to marine life, while others may be beneficial.

(a) Several varieties of bacteria have been found living on plastic fragments in seawater.
(b) Some forms of plastic have been proven to be beneficial to marine life in small amounts.

Vocabulary In the context of the passage, ☐ means _____.

1 **drawn**	(a) attracted	(b) described	(c) challenged	(d) delivered
2 **erected**	(a) demonstrated	(b) exposed	(c) established	(d) replicated
3 **detected**	(a) attached	(b) noticed	(c) comprehended	(d) pursued

지문을 읽고 문제에 알맞은 답을 고르세요.

VOLCANIC ERUPTIONS RESPONSIBLE FOR EARTH'S FIRST MASS EXTINCTION

Researchers have found evidence that volcanoes may have caused the oldest-known mass extinction on Earth. This extinction event lasted for thousands of years and extinguished nearly all species on the planet roughly 250 million years ago.

The mass extinction has been known about for years, but its causes have always been based on assumptions. This is the first time that scientists have collected convincing physical evidence in support of a theory. What they have found is the presence of high mercury in rocks from the period.

The study's lead author, Jun Shen, says that large eruptions often release a lot of mercury into the atmosphere through volcanic gases and the burning of organic material. In this case, when the mercury returned to the surface in falling rain, it was preserved in sediment layers.

According to the researchers, continual volcanic eruptions occurring in quick succession heated the atmosphere and contaminated it with mercury. The resulting global warming and acid rain damaged the environment and its inhabitants, leaving little chance for adaptation or recovery and causing species to disappear.

The findings offer a warning about releasing carbon dioxide into the atmosphere. Scientists suggest that human-caused global warming could have a similar outcome.

---

04 What is the article mainly about?

   (a) the causes of large volcanic eruptions
   (b) how volcanoes led to mass extinctions

05 Which is true about the mercury released by the volcanoes?

   (a) It came back to the surface with rain.
   (b) It remained in the atmosphere for many years.

06 Why most likely are scientists concerned about the release of so much carbon dioxide?

   (a) It could result in more volcanic activity.
   (b) It could cause widespread destruction.

Vocabulary In the context of the passage, ☐ means _____.

4 **assumptions**	(a) facts	(b) guesses	(c) thoughts	(d) beliefs
5 **damaged**	(a) affected	(b) stressed	(c) injured	(d) burdened

HOW THE PHRASE *HOLD YOUR HORSES* CAME ABOUT

Some idioms functioned as literal phrases before they ultimately got non-literal meanings. One of these is *hold your horses*, a common idiom that people use to tell someone to wait, slow down, or calm down.

The literal meaning of the phrase can be found in old literature in a variety of cultures. In the *Iliad*, the prolific author Homer wrote "Hold your horses!" as a command to one of the characters who was driving his chariot wildly during a race. In Latin literature, sources refer to the need for soldiers to keep their horses under control during the loud sounds of battle.

In the 1600s, it was used when criminals were trampled by horses as punishment for their crimes. In such cases, the executioner would tell the men to hold their horses while the criminal was tied to the ground in preparation for his ruthless punishment.

The imperative's non-literal meaning originated in America in the 19th century. At first, it was written "hold your hosses" using the old slang term for horse. One of the first idiomatic usages appeared in the New Orleans newspaper *Picayune* in 1844. Telling someone he needed to calm down and not get upset, the author wrote "Oh, hold your horses".

---

07 How did Homer use the literal use of phrase?

(a) as a directive to a racing chariot driver
(b) as a command to soldiers on the battlefield

08 Based on the article, what was not a situation in which the phrase *hold your horses* was used prior to the 19th century?

(a) while preparing to mete out the penalty for a crime
(b) when halting a scheduled execution at the last minute

09 What was written in the *Picayune* in 1844?

(a) an early figurative use of an expression
(b) the first use of a popular slang term

Vocabulary In the context of the passage, ☐ means _____ .

6 **prolific**	(a) productive	(b) amicable	(c) descriptive	(d) loquacious
7 **ruthless**	(a) implacable	(b) weak	(c) harsh	(d) vacuous

SCIENTISTS TRACK ANCIENT WHALE MIGRATION ROUTES

A recent study has revealed that humpback and grey whales still follow patterns of migration that originated five million years ago. The new study, as described in *Proceedings of the National Academy of Sciences*, relied on barnacle fossils to track the routes of ancient whale migrations.

Barnacles are sea creatures that attach themselves to objects, including whales. They are easier to study than whale fossils because they are found in greater quantities.

As barnacles grow, their shells absorb oxygen isotopes from the surrounding water. These isotopes are significant because they leave chemical traces in barnacle shells, indicating where the barnacles have been. This helps scientists trace the movements over time of not just the barnacles but also the whales to which they were once attached.

When scientists mapped the routes from these fossils, they discovered that they were almost identical to current whale migration routes. The final conclusion of the study was that seasonal migration patterns have remained largely unchanged for millions of years.

Future research will attempt to use the same technique to detect migration patterns from further in the past. The researchers also hope to use it to study other whale populations.

10 What did the study find out?

(a) that whale migration routes have not changed in millions of years
(b) that whale fossils reveal how ancient sea creatures migrated

11 What is the significance of isotopes?

(a) They reveal the age of the barnacle shell fossils.
(b) They help reconstruct whale movements over time.

12 What will future studies focus on?

(a) differentiating ancient and modern whales
(b) determining even older migration patterns

정답·해석·해설 p.22

Vocabulary In the context of the passage, ☐ means _____ .   Vocabulary 정답·해석 p.25

| 8 **quantities** | (a) capacities | (b) sizes | (c) shortages | (d) numbers |
| 9 **conclusion** | (a) goal | (b) decision | (c) result | (d) completion |

1·7

STUDY EXAMINES RELATIONSHIP BETWEEN TEMPERATURE AND PERFORMANCE

According to a recent academic study conducted at Technical University Berlin in Germany, the cognitive performance of men and women differs depending on variations in room temperature. The study found that at higher temperatures, women showed an improvement in performance while men's abilities were diminished. Moreover, the increase in female performance was more noticeable than the decrease in male performance.

In the study, the researchers compared the effectiveness of more than 500 men and women in carrying out various tasks. The subjects were all students recruited online from universities in Berlin. As university students generally possess similar cognitive skills, this allowed researchers to gather a relatively homogenous group of participants. Around 60 percent of the students were male and 40 percent were female. They were compensated based on how well they carried out the tasks.

Within a laboratory setting, the selected participants were given identical mental tasks to work on to test how well they performed under different conditions. In the math task, they were asked to add up five numbers without using a calculator. In the verbal task, they were given ten letters of the alphabet and told to create as many words as they could.

The only difference between the various sessions was temperature. The researchers alternated the temperature between 16 and 33 degrees Celsius, so some people performed in cooler or warmer conditions compared to those in other groups. For every increase of one degree Celsius, there was a 1.76 percent increase in correct answers by women on the math task, and a 1.03 percent jump in correct answers on the verbal task. In contrast, a 1-degree temperature increase resulted in a 0.63 and 0.6 percent decrease in men's performance on the math and verbal tasks, respectively.

Although the performance differences were not large, the findings suggest that the gender-based "battles of the thermostat" that commonly occur in offices should not revolve around individual preferences or subjective notions of comfort. Rather, there may be an objective basis for selecting the ideal workplace temperature. The researchers propose that wherever the ratio of men to women is balanced, the optimal temperature should be warmer than is currently practiced.

1. What did the researchers find out?

   (a) that temperature affects men and women differently
   (b) that there is an ideal climate for best cognitive performance
   (c) that cognitive performance in men and women is the same
   (d) that men and women have different body temperatures

2. What is true of the experiment's participants?

   (a) Half were women and half were men.
   (b) Some of them worked at the laboratory.
   (c) They all had about the same level of cognition.
   (d) They were all students at Technical University Berlin.

3. How did researchers analyze the participants in the study?

   (a) by making them do certain tasks at the same time
   (b) by having them complete math tasks without a calculator
   (c) by letting them do certain tasks separately or in groups
   (d) by asking them to recite the alphabet ten times

4. When did the male participants' performance in math drop by 0.63 percent?

   (a) after the temperature was increased by 1.76 degrees
   (b) once the temperature dropped below a certain level
   (c) during the time the temperature was at 16 degrees
   (d) when the temperature had gone up by 1 degree

5. What would the researchers probably recommend for workplaces with equal numbers of men and women?

   (a) changing the thermostat often
   (b) increasing the temperature
   (c) using personal space heaters
   (d) decreasing the temperature

6. In the context of the passage, diminished means _____.

   (a) reduced
   (b) increased
   (c) exhausted
   (d) condensed

7. In the context of the passage, compensated means _____.

   (a) recommended
   (b) thanked
   (c) rewarded
   (d) appreciated

MXENE INK USED TO PRINT ENERGY CONDUCTING DEVICES

Researchers have discovered that the ink MXene has conductive properties that are far superior to other forms of ink. It can therefore be used to print flexible electrical components for the transfer or storage of energy, such as supercapacitors, in any size or shape. MXene is also more versatile than other forms of conductive ink and can be used for a potentially far greater range of purposes.

All conductive inks are able to conduct electricity, which means that flexible materials like paper can become a base for electronics if they are printed with conductive ink. These inks are already used to make radiofrequency identification tags, print circuit boards on portable devices, and embed radio antennas onto car windows. MXene is expected to deliver huge advancements in several key areas. For instance, it is more conductive, is functional on a wider range of surfaces, and can be integrated into the manufacturing processes of energy components.

What makes MXene truly unique is that it does not require a chemical additive to hold its ink particles together. Whereas other inks require additional treatments before and after printing, MXene can be mixed with water and other organic liquids without any concurrent loss of quality or of conductivity. For this reason, it can dry quickly without the need for additional processing.

MXene is also more flexible, as its individual layers are just a few atoms thick, allowing a large number of them to be packed tightly together. Already, researchers have successfully used MXene to print on paper, plastic, and glass. They have demonstrated not only that MXene can be printed in lines of consistent thickness but also that by varying the thickness of the lines, they can control MXene's conductivity. This allows MXene printouts to surpass the conductivity of all other carbon-based conductive inks.

Given these considerations, MXene is an extremely versatile product. The MXene levels in the ink can even be adjusted to suit different kinds of inkjet printers, extending their applicability to commercial devices found in homes and offices. Moreover, direct ink printing techniques that use MXene should allow for easy customization, reductions in material waste, and mass production of both MXene printouts and associated energy storage devices.

8. What is the article all about?

    (a) a device made from a new ink-based material

    (b) an example of a miniature electronic tool

    (c) a substance that electricity can pass through

    (d) a process for manufacturing ink

9. Based on the article, how are conductive inks currently being used?

    (a) to embed supercapacitors in automobiles

    (b) to make radiofrequency identification labels

    (c) to print circuit boards on computers

    (d) to add antennas to radio towers

10. How is MXene different from other conductive inks?

    (a) It dissolves in liquid.

    (b) It takes less time to dry.

    (c) It lasts longer before fading.

    (d) It consumes less material.

11. How can lines of MXene be altered to control their conductivity?

    (a) by varying their thickness

    (b) by increasing their length

    (c) by changing their color

    (d) by increasing their longevity

12. What shows that MXene is highly versatile?

    (a) It can lower energy use in homes.

    (b) It can be produced using household chemicals.

    (c) It can reduce the amount of ink used in offices.

    (d) It can be modified for common inkjet printers.

13. In the context of the passage, advancements means _____.

    (a) payments

    (b) requests

    (c) movements

    (d) improvements

14. In the context of the passage, surpass means _____.

    (a) master

    (b) further

    (c) outdo

    (d) overcome

CHILDREN'S EATING HABITS DETERMINED BY SUPPLY

A study has found that children eat more of the foods they don't like if they are told the foods are limited in quantity. They are also more likely to want to do certain activities if they believe those activities will be restricted.

Researchers Michal Maimaran and Yuval Salant say they were motivated to conduct the study by a personal experience they had. While dining out at a sushi restaurant, they witnessed their children expressing an unusual preference for the thin slices of avocado served in small amounts with some dishes. The researchers wondered whether the limited availability of the avocado had somehow increased its desirability. To explore this idea, they administered a series of studies among 51 preschool children.

In the studies, each child was invited to play with some toy blocks before being directed to a plate of carrots. Some children were given just 10 minutes to play with the blocks, while others were told they could play as long as they liked. Similarly, some were informed that they could have only one plate of carrots, while others were told they could have as many as they wanted.

What the researchers discovered is that children who were asked to limit their play time spent an average of one-and-a-half minutes more with the blocks. And among those who believed the carrots were limited, 50 percent ate the entire plate versus 35 percent in the other group. Moreover, 96 percent of the kids in the group that believed the carrots were limited said the carrots tasted "yummy" compared to just 67 percent in the other group. Two succeeding studies were conducted, offering the children a choice between carrots and other snacks, with limits only on carrots, and similar behaviors were manifested.

The psychology behind the children's behavior is not yet precisely understood. Nevertheless, it has interesting implications for parents. For instance, conventional wisdom states that parents should encourage children to eat more healthy foods like fruits and vegetables and discourage them from eating less healthy foods like chips, cookies, and candy. However, the study suggests that parents will have more success by artificially limiting quantities of healthy food and removing limits on unhealthy food.

15. What is the topic of the article?

(a) why children prefer to eat unhealthy food
(b) which food choices lead to unhealthy outcomes
(c) what parents can do to control children's diets
(d) how restrictions affect children's food choices

16. What prompted the researchers to carry out the study?

(a) their personal observations
(b) their experience with school food
(c) their children's health issues
(d) their dining habits as children

17. How did the researchers analyze the eating habits of children?

(a) by allowing all the children to eat and play as much as they wanted
(b) by asking children to rate foods and toys from a list
(c) by giving some children limitations on food and play
(d) by encouraging kids to eat and play together

18. Which is true about the children's responses in the study?

(a) They spent less time playing when they were hungry.
(b) Half of the ones given restrictions ate all their vegetables.
(c) They ate more carrots when allowed to play afterwards.
(d) All of those who ate the carrots said they enjoyed them.

19. Based on the passage, which of the following would be one way of encouraging healthy eating?

(a) serving food following playtime
(b) taking away limits on unhealthy food
(c) rewarding good behavior with healthy food
(d) removing all snack food items from home

20. In the context of the passage, administered means _____.

(a) calculated
(b) contributed
(c) authorized
(d) performed

21. In the context of the passage, manifested means _____.

(a) proved
(b) hidden
(c) exhibited
(d) declared

VIRTUAL REALITY GAMING GROWS
BUT STILL FACES REAL CHALLENGES

The Virtual Reality (VR) gaming industry is finally making some gains in the gaming market. After seeing a slow start and investing billions of dollars, VR companies are gradually starting to attract more players.

VR players get a unique experience because, unlike traditional video games, VR games allow the person to see the game from his or her own perspective. In other words, the player is a key character in the game and can alter the environment from within the game.

However, the industry still has a long way to go. According to market research by SuperData, VR gaming accounts for less than 1 percent of the total gaming market. Moreover, few VR games generated more than a million dollars in sales prior to the past few years. Among the recent exceptions was the sensation *The Walking Dead: Saints and Sinners*, which led all VR games at $29 million in 2020. Still, in contrast, the conventional game series *Call of Duty* generated $3 billion in revenue in 2020.

Clearly, the VR industry must continue to attract more members of the gaming community, of which less than a third report owning a VR system. One way of doing this is to continue to improve hardware and software while markedly reducing prices. Facebook, which purchased the rights to Oculus VR headsets from their creator in 2014, introduced Oculus Quest for $399 and later the more advanced Quest 2 for $299, which is expected to boost sales.

While the cost of VR headsets may not be a drawback in the future, some issues may not be as easy to overcome. One is that some people get motion sickness or nausea while playing VR games. For some people, such as those with epilepsy, it can even result in seizures.

Nonetheless, experts anticipate that the VR market will grow tremendously as long as more best-selling game series, such as *Assassin's Creed*, enter the VR platform. Also, they emphasize that VR is still early in its evolution with endless opportunities to create more intimate and realistic gaming experiences that most gamers will eventually try out and embrace.

22. According to the article, what does VR gaming allow the player to do?

(a) alternate between VR and traditional views
(b) change the surroundings from inside the game
(c) view the game from another player's perspective
(d) play the game through multiple characters

23. What characterizes the revenue that *Call of Duty* produced?

(a) It set a record for profits from a single game series.
(b) It first surpassed three billion dollars in 2020.
(c) It was more than the revenue of all video games combined.
(d) It far exceeded that of the top-selling VR game.

24. According to the article, what did Facebook do in 2014?

(a) introduced a new and improved headset
(b) reduced the price of their Quest products
(c) bought the license to use a headset brand
(d) invested in better software and hardware

25. Why most likely will some gamers avoid VR in the future?

(a) They may not be willing to pay for the rising costs.
(b) They will still prefer to play their favorite traditional games.
(c) They might be concerned for their physical well-being.
(d) They will embrace less realistic gaming experiences.

26. What do experts indicate about the future VR market?

(a) It will most likely never reach its full potential.
(b) It will cause conventional game platforms to become obsolete.
(c) It will attract new investors to develop better VR technology.
(d) It will need to include more games that are popular with players.

27. In the context of the passage, sensation means _____.

(a) event
(b) hit
(c) bet
(d) flop

28. In the context of the passage, markedly means _____.

(a) noticeably
(b) predictably
(c) successfully
(d) understandably

STUDY REVEALS FINDINGS ABOUT
GENERATIONAL ATTITUDES TOWARD RELIGION

A research team led by author and psychology professor Jean M. Twenge discovered that millennials in the US may be the least religious generation not only in the last six decades, but possibly in the nation's history. This change may be due to a larger cultural shift that has occurred in American society in recent decades.

The scope of data researchers analyzed for the study is unprecedented in scale. In all, researchers from three universities incorporated information from four nationally representative surveys of US teenagers taken between 1966 and 2014. The study is also unique for having examined members of younger age groups than previous studies and, unlike most polls on religion, for considering the larger cultural context within which religious attitudes have changed.

A sampling of the study's findings reveals a steady decline in religious belief among young people, most marked among members of the millennial generation, or those born between the early 1980s and late-1990s. Compared to the 1970s, double the number of people in this age bracket have never attended religious services, while the majority of them consider religion to be "not important at all." Compared to the early 1980s, three times as many millennial college students answered "none" when asked what religion they belong to. And compared to the 1990s, 20 percent fewer of these students described themselves as interested in spirituality, suggesting that they have not replaced participation in organized religion with a general spiritual practice.

Overall, millennials are less spiritual, less likely to say that religion is personally important, and less religious than earlier generations were at the same age. They are also more likely to abandon religion before reaching adulthood, with an increasing number not raised with religion at all. In general, they do not consider religion to be a part of their regular lives.

According to Twenge, the trend away from religion may be better understood from the perspective of cultural change. For instance, a notable shift toward individualism has swept through American society since the 1970s. As a result, young people are more likely to have a sense of greater self-importance and prioritize themselves over groups to which they belong, such as communities of citizens, corporations, or institutions.

29. What did the study find out about millennials?

(a) They are open to experiencing other religions.
(b) They are less religious than their elders.
(c) They have unique views about spirituality.
(d) They form movements against organized religion.

30. How is Twenge's study different from others before it?

(a) It focuses on adolescents.
(b) It includes the results of online polls.
(c) It examines the context of changes.
(d) It uses publicly available data.

31. Which does NOT describe the millennial generation?

(a) They are less spiritual than 1990s college students.
(b) Half of them have never attended any religious services.
(c) Three times as many of them identify as irreligious than students in the 80s.
(d) The majority of them see no value in the institution of religion.

32. What does the article suggest about the childhood of millennials?

(a) They were generally more religious as children.
(b) Their schools instructed them in religious practice.
(c) They rebelled against their parents' beliefs.
(d) Their parents did not practice a religion at home.

33. Based on the article, what did people start to do in the 1970s?

(a) focus more on their individual concerns
(b) learn about cultures other than their own
(c) study psychological concepts like the self
(d) lose trust in large institutions like religion

34. In the context of the passage, scope means _____.

(a) space
(b) limit
(c) resource
(d) range

35. In the context of the passage, regular means _____.

(a) normal
(b) monotonous
(c) atypical
(d) reliable

정답·해석·해설 p.25

G-TELP 빈출 어휘

PART 2에서 선별한 다음의 지텔프 빈출 어휘들을 암기한 후 퀴즈로 확인해보세요.

classify v. 분류하다

retrieve v. 회수하다, 탐색하다

examination n. 조사, 검토

separate adj. 구분된, 별개의

confirm v. 입증하다

ecosystem n. 생태계

hypothesis n. 가설

unprecedented adj. 전례 없는

depict v. 묘사하다

surface n. 표면

accumulate v. 쌓다, 축적하다

harmful adj. 해로운

extinction n. 멸종

release v. 방출하다

atmosphere n. 대기

sediment n. 퇴적

contaminate v. 오염시키다

phrase n. 말, 구절

literal adj. 문자 그대로의

ultimately adv. 궁극적으로

command n. 명령

literature n. 문학

criminal n. 범인, 범죄자

punishment n. 형벌, 처벌

preparation n. 준비, 대비

ruthless adj. 무자비한

usage n. 용법, 사용

ancient adj. 고대의

fossil n. 화석

absorb v. 흡수하다

oxygen n. 산소

population n. 개체, 인구

cognitive adj. 인지의

diminish v. 낮아지다

Quiz 각 단어의 알맞은 뜻을 찾아 연결하세요.

01	ecosystem	ⓐ 형벌, 처벌	06	ancient	ⓗ 준비, 대비
		ⓑ 인지의			ⓘ 방출하다
02	command	ⓒ 명령	07	confirm	ⓙ 고대의
		ⓓ 흡수하다			ⓚ 입증하다
03	extinction	ⓔ 생태계	08	population	ⓛ 무자비한
		ⓕ 멸종			
04	punishment		09	unprecedented	ⓜ 개체, 인구
		ⓖ 낮아지다			ⓝ 전례 없는
05	cognitive		10	preparation	

정답 01 ⓔ 02 ⓒ 03 ⓕ 04 ⓐ 05 ⓑ 06 ⓙ 07 ⓚ 08 ⓜ 09 ⓝ 10 ⓗ

possess v. 가지다, 소유하다

compensate v. 보상하다

laboratory n. 실험실

notion n. 의견, 개념

ideal adj. 이상적인

climate n. 기후, 날씨

superior adj. 우수한

flexible adj. 유연한

versatile adj. 다용도의

portable adj. 휴대용의

manufacture v. 제작하다

organic adj. 유기의

consistent adj. 일관된

substance n. 물질

alter v. 변형하다

modify v. 조정하다, 변경하다

supply n. 지급량 v. 공급하다

witness v. 목격하다

inform v. 통지하다

average n. 평균

behavior n. 행동, 태도

encourage v. 장려하다

discourage v. 막다, 말리다

rate v. 순위를 매기다, 평가하다

attract v. 끌어모으다

generate v. 창출하다, 만들어 내다

anticipate v. 예상하다

evolution n. 발전, 진전

millennial n. 밀레니얼 세대

poll n. 여론 조사

abandon v. 버리다, 떠나다

perspective n. 관점

notable adj. 눈에 띄는, 유명한

prioritize v. 우선시하다

Quiz 각 단어의 알맞은 뜻을 찾아 연결하세요.

01 superior	ⓐ 밀레니얼 세대		06 anticipate	ⓗ 장려하다	
02 abandon	ⓑ 평균		07 notable	ⓘ 눈에 띄는, 유명한	
03 laboratory	ⓒ 물질		08 climate	ⓙ 관점	
04 millennial	ⓓ 우수한		09 perspective	ⓚ 일관된	
05 average	ⓔ 버리다, 떠나다		10 versatile	ⓛ 다용도의	
	ⓕ 끌어모으다			ⓜ 기후, 날씨	
	ⓖ 실험실			ⓝ 예상하다	

정답 01 ⓓ 02 ⓔ 03 ⓖ 04 ⓐ 05 ⓑ 06 ⓝ 07 ⓘ 08 ⓜ 09 ⓙ 10 ⓛ

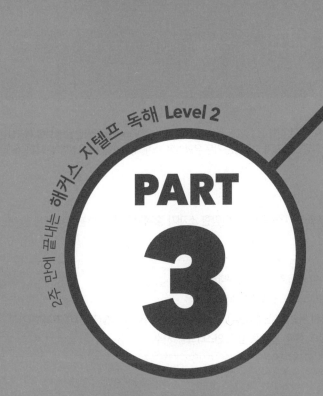

2주 만에 끝내는 해커스 지텔프 독해 Level 2

PART 3

지식 백과

Encyclopedia Article

PART 3 지식 백과 Encyclopedia Article

PART 3에서는 인문학, 사회 과학, 자연 과학 등 다양한 분야의 한 가지 소재를 소개하고 관련된 정보를 제공하는 백과사전식 지문이 출제된다. 4개 파트 중에서 가장 다양한 소재가 출제되는 지문 유형이며, 소재의 정의와 기원, 소재의 특징 등을 묻는 문제가 출제된다.

─◉ 출제 토픽

역사적 사건, 동식물, 스포츠, 대중문화 등 다양한 소재가 출제되지만, 대부분 우리에게 친숙한 것에 대해 출제되는 편이다.

> ・인문학   캘리포니아 골드 러시(역사), 쿠마리(종교)
> ・사회 과학   스톤헨지(고고학), 밴드왜건 효과(심리학)
> **빈출** ・자연 과학   딥 블루(AI 기술), 백반증(건강), 침팬지, 천산갑(동물), 싱크홀(자연), 오로라 현상(지구 과학)
> ・대중문화   디즈니랜드, 헤나, 노래방, 검도, 인스타그램, 자수

─◉ 문제 유형

지문의 주제를 묻는 문제나 소재의 정의를 묻는 문제가 주로 첫 번째 문제로 출제된다. 간혹 PART 1에서 자주 출제되는 유명한 이유를 묻는 문제가 출제되기도 하며, 목적 문제는 출제되지 않는다.

주제	지문의 주제를 묻는다. **What is the article mainly about?** 지문의 주제는 무엇인가?
특정세부사항	소재의 정의, 기원, 특징, 유명한 이유 등 지문에서 언급된 세부사항을 묻는다. **When** was the first rugby game played? 최초의 럭비 시합은 언제 시행되었는가?
Not/True	소재에 대해 언급된 것에 대해 사실이거나 사실이 아닌 것을 묻는다. What is **true** about the Great Wall of China today? 오늘날 중국의 만리장성에 대해 사실인 것은?
추론	소재에 대한 설명을 통해 추론할 수 있는 것을 묻는다. Why **most likely** is tourism causing problems for Chichen Itza? 왜 관광 산업이 치첸이트사에 문제를 일으키고 있는 것 같은가?
어휘	지문의 문맥에서 밑줄 어휘의 유의어가 무엇인지를 묻는다. In the context of the passage, **assumption** means _____. 지문의 문맥에서, 'assumption'은 -을 의미한다.

─◉ 핵심 전략

1. '정의 → 기원 → 특징'의 패턴화된 흐름에서 출제되는 빈출 문제들을 알아두어야 한다.

2. 기원, 구성, 특징을 설명하는 내용은 관련 표현을 익혀두면 쉽게 찾을 수 있다.

3. 첫 단락에서 소재의 정의를 확인해두면 지문의 전반적인 내용을 이해할 때 도움이 된다.

지문 흐름	흐름에 따른 빈출 문제

알레르기

알레르기란 어떤 종류의 물질을 섭취하거나 접촉했을 때 나타나는 몸의 반응으로, 몸의 면역 체계가 과민 반응을 보일 때 일어난다.

알레르기의 어원은 그리스어 'allos'와 'ergon'에서 유래했으며, '이상한 반응'이라는 뜻이다. 알레르기 질환은 일반적으로 개체 요인과 환경 요인으로 인해 발생한다. 개체 요인에는 유전, 성별, 나이 등이 있으며, 유전적 요인이 가장 큰 영향을 끼치는 것으로 알려진다.

대표적인 질환으로는 알레르기 비염, 기관지 천식, 아토피 피부염이 있다. 알레르기 비염은 재채기, 콧물, 코막힘 등이 증상이며 미국 인구의 11퍼센트가 앓고 있다. 기관지 천식은 약 3퍼센트의 인구가 앓고 있으며, 기관지가 수축하고 기침 및 호흡 곤란 증상이 발생하는 질환이다. 아토피 피부염은 약 9퍼센트의 인구가 앓고 있는 가려움증을 동반한 피부염으로 최근에는 아이들에게 많이 나타나고 있다.

생활 환경의 변화로 인해 알레르기로 병원을 찾는 사람이 많아지고 있다. 이에 따라, 공중 생물학자들은 공기 중에 부유하는 세균 등을 연구하며 알레르기의 요인을 없앨 수 있는 방법을 찾고 있다. 알레르기 반응을 낮춘 저알레르기 분유 등도 역시 개발되고 있으며, 알레르기에 관한 연구는 계속되고 있다.

알레르기는 완치되기 어렵고, 원인이 되는 물질에 노출되는 것을 피하거나, 노출을 줄이는 방법이 현재로서는 최선이다. 약물 치료도 가능하지만, 전문가와 상담하여 적절한 치료를 하는 것이 중요하다.

정의

소재의 정의를 묻는 문제가 주로 출제된다.
ex What is an allergy?
알레르기란 무엇인가?

기원 및 발생 요인

소재의 기원 및 발생 요인을 묻는 문제가 출제된다.
ex What does the origin of its name suggest?
알레르기의 어원은 무엇을 나타내는가?

소재에 대해 사실인 것을 묻는 문제가 출제된다.
ex What is true about the risk factors of allergies?
알레르기의 위험 요인에 대해 사실인 것은?

특징 1: 종류

소재에 대한 세부적인 내용을 묻는 문제가 출제된다.
ex What symptoms will a person who is suffering from asthma have?
천식을 앓는 사람은 무슨 증상을 가질 것인가?

특징 2: 오늘날 변화

소재의 최근 특징에 대해 묻는 문제가 출제된다.
ex Why do people visit the hospital more often today?
요즘 사람들은 왜 병원을 더 자주 찾는가?

특징 3: 치료법

세부내용에 대해 추론하는 문제가 출제된다.
ex What most likely is not one of the treatments for allergies?
알레르기 치료법 중 하나가 아닌 것은 무엇인 것 같은가?

1. 기원

① **originate from**   ~에서 비롯되다

The bridge **originated from** the Victorian era.

그 다리는 빅토리아 시대에서 비롯되었다.

② **date back to**   ~까지 거슬러 올라가다

The oldest structures in Angkor Wat **date back to** the 12th century.

앙코르와트의 가장 오래된 건축물은 12세기까지 거슬러 올라간다.

③ **derive from**   ~에서 유래하다

The name Arthur's Seat **derives from** the legend of King Arthur.

아서시트라는 이름은 아서왕의 전설에서 유래한다.

2. 구성

④ **be made up of**   ~으로 구성되다

The Acropolis **is made up of** palaces, temples, and monuments.

아크로폴리스는 궁전, 신전, 그리고 기념비로 구성되어 있다.

⑤ **be composed of**   ~으로 이루어지다

The dish **is composed of** fresh raw fish, citrus juices, and some spice.

그 요리는 신선한 생선회, 감귤 주스, 그리고 약간의 양념으로 이루어져 있다.

3. 특징

⑥ **be characterized by**   ~으로 특징지어지다

The landscape surrounding the monument **is characterized by** flat plains and dry bush.

기념비를 둘러싼 지형은 평평한 평원과 마른 덤불로 특징지어진다.

⑦ **be described as**   ~으로 묘사되다

Picasso's *Guernica* **is described as** the greatest anti-war painting of all time.

피카소의 「게르니카」는 역사상 가장 위대한 반전 그림으로 묘사된다.

1. 기원 및 소개

exist v. 존재하다, 나타나다

remain v. 남다, 계속 ~이다 n. 유적, 화석

intrigue v. 호기심을 불러일으키다

trigger v. 촉발시키다 n. 계기, 방아쇠

report v. 발표하다

term n. 용어

origin n. 기원, 근원

translate v. 번역되다, 바뀌다

involve v. 포함하다, 관련시키다

theory n. 이론, 학설

status n. 신분, 지위

common adj. 흔한, 공통의

tradition n. 전통

historical adj. 역사상의

2. 구성 및 과정

include v. 포함하다

contain v. 포함하다, 함유하다

consist v. 이루어지다

substance n. 물질

civilization n. 문명 (사회)

conflict n. 갈등, 충돌

exchange v. 교환하다 n. 교환

attach v. 붙이다, 첨부하다

appear v. 나타나다, ~인 것 같다

lead v. 이끌다, 하게 되다

document n. 서류, 문서 v. 기록하다

phase n. 단계, 시기

3. 특징 및 세부사항

unique adj. 독특한

natural adj. 자연의

environment n. 환경

habitat n. 서식지

pollution n. 오염, 공해

descendant n. 자손, 후손

heritage n. 유산

thrive v. 번창하다

utilize v. 활용하다

structure n. 구조, 건축물

material n. 직물, 재료

complex adj. 복잡한

several adj. 몇몇의

abundant adj. 풍부한

benefit n. 혜택, 이득 v. 혜택을 받다

consistent adj. 한결같은, 변함없는

approximate adj. 거의 정확한, 근사치의

distinguish v. 구별하다, 차이를 보이다

GRAMMY AWARDS

지문 흐름

1 The Grammy Awards is an event held each year, during which prizes are given by the Recording Academy for achievements in the music industry. **American music executives created it to acknowledge not just the acclaimed musicians whose popularity sells records but also the other professionals who work behind the scenes.**

→ 1번 키워드

정의 및 기원

2 The Gramophone Awards, as they were originally known, were first held in 1959, with **a total of 28 prizes given out. That number has fluctuated over the years as new genres and categories have emerged**. Currently, over 75 awards are presented in over 25 fields.

→ 2번 키워드

변화

3 The Grammy selection process begins with Academy members choosing qualifying entries, usually from recordings released in the preceding year. Then, the members determine which categories the recordings belong to. These include specific genres, technical aspects of production, and the best album of the year, as well as categories for individuals who have made important contributions. Lastly, **voting members choose five nominees, and the eventual winner, but they only judge entries in categories in which they have expertise**.

→ 3번 키워드

특징 1:
선정 과정

4 Winners are announced during a televised ceremony that includes performances by popular artists. They receive a handmade, gold-plated statue aptly shaped like a gramophone, an old-fashioned record player. **Since 1997, the Recording Academy has also held a separate Latin Grammys event to recognize recordings in Spanish and Portuguese.**

→ 4번 키워드

특징 2:
시상식

5번 키워드 →

5 Despite comprehensive category changes in 2012, viewership of the Grammys has largely declined. **Many criticize it for favoring commercial achievement rather than artistic ability.** Still, receiving a nomination or a prize has usually resulted in greater record sales and wider recognition for an artist.

특징 3:
현황

그래미 시상식이 처음에 제정되었을 때 목적을 묻고 있으므로, 정의 및 기원을 언급하는 1단락에서 단서를 찾는다.

1. What was an aim of the Grammy Awards when it was first created ?

   (a) to promote specific genres of music

   (b) to capitalize on music's growing popularity

   (c) to recognize figures working in the background

   (d) to reward top-performing music executives

그래미 시상식에 대해 변한 것을 묻고 있으므로, 변화를 언급하는 2단락에서 단서를 찾는다.

2. Based on the article, what about the Grammy Awards has changed over the years ?

   (a) the number of prizes given out

   (b) the type of trophy winners receive

   (c) the length of the televised broadcast

   (d) the network that airs the ceremony

그래미상 선정 과정에 대해 사실인 것을 묻고 있으므로, 선정 과정을 언급하는 3단락에서 단서를 찾는다.

3. Which is true about the Grammy selection process ?

   (a) Artists must release a set number of songs to qualify.

   (b) Judges must be experts in the categories they evaluate.

   (c) Nominees cannot appear in more than four categories.

   (d) Votes must be counted by a committee of members.

1990년대에 레코딩 아카데미가 한 것을 묻고 있으므로, 질문의 키워드 In the 1990s가 Since 1997로 언급된 4단락에서 단서를 찾는다.

4. In the 1990s , what did the Recording Academy do?

   (a) broadcasted in multiple languages

   (b) changed the design of a trophy

   (c) increased the number of nominees

   (d) introduced a new type of Grammy Award

그래미 시상식의 인기 하락의 원인을 묻고 있으므로, 질문의 키워드 declining popularity가 viewership ~ declined로 paraphrasing되어 언급된 5단락에서 단서를 찾는다.

5. What could be the reason for the Grammy Awards' declining popularity ?

   (a) Recording companies are spending less money on it.

   (b) The awards value record sales more than talent.

   (c) Recognition in the Grammys is no longer rewarding.

   (d) The categories do not reflect recent changes in music.

6. In the context of the passage, contributions means _____.

   (a) quantities

   (b) donations

   (c) improvements

   (d) accomplishments

7. In the context of the passage, aptly means _____.

   (a) sufficiently

   (b) perfectly

   (c) fittingly

   (d) officially

해석 및 해설 뒷장에서 확인하기 ➡

그래미 시상식

1 그래미 시상식은 매년 개최되는 행사로, 이때 음반 업계의 성취에 대한 상이 레코딩 아카데미에 의해 수여된다. [1]인기가 음반을 팔리게 하는 호평받는 음악가들뿐만 아니라 배후에서 일하는 다른 전문가들도 인정해주기 위해 미국의 음악계 중역들이 이를 제정했다.

2 원래 그라모폰 시상식이라고 알려져 있었던 이 시상식은 1959년에 처음 개최되었고, [2]총 28개의 상이 시상되었다. 이 숫자는 새로운 장르와 카테고리가 등장하면서 수년간 변동을 거듭했다. 현재, 75개가 넘는 상이 25개가 넘는 분야에서 수여되고 있다.

3 그래미상의 선정 과정은 아카데미 회원들이 보통 전년에 발표된 음반에서 자격이 되는 출품작들을 선택하는 것으로 시작한다. 그다음, 회원들은 그 음반들이 어떤 카테고리에 속하는지 결정한다. 이는 특정 장르, 저작물의 기술적인 측면, 그리고 올해의 앨범에 더하여, 중요한 공헌을 한 개인을 위한 카테고리를 포함한다. 마지막으로, [3]투표하는 회원들은 다섯 후보와 최종적인 수상자를 선택하는데, 하지만 그들은 오직 자신이 전문 지식을 가진 카테고리의 출품작들만 심사한다.

4 수상자들은 텔레비전으로 방송되는 유명한 예술가들에 의한 공연을 포함한 시상식에서 발표된다. 그들은 옛날 전축인 축음기 모양으로 적절히 만들어진 수제 도금 조각상을 받는다. [4]1997년 이래로, 레코딩 아카데미는 스페인어와 포르투갈어로 발매되는 음반도 표창하기 위해 별도의 라틴 그래미 시상식도 개최해왔다.

5 2012년의 종합적인 카테고리의 변화에도 불구하고, 그래미 시상식의 시청률은 크게 하락했다. [5]많은 사람들은 예술적 능력보다는 오히려 상업적 성과를 장려한다고 그것을 비판한다. 그래도, 수상 후보 지명이나 상을 받는 것은 보통 더 나은 음반 판매와 예술가에 대한 더 큰 인정으로 이어져왔다.

어휘 achievement n. 성취, 업적 executive n. 중역, 임원 acknowledge v. 인정하다, 감사를 표하다 fluctuate v. 변동을 거듭하다 emerge v. 등장하다, 나오다 field n. 분야 entry n. 출품작, 입장 technical adj. 기술적인 aspect n. 측면, 양상 contribution n. 공헌, 기여 nominee n. 후보 expertise n. 전문 지식 televised adj. 텔레비전으로 방송되는 gold-plated adj. 도금된 aptly adv. 적절히 gramophone n. 축음기 old-fashioned adj. 옛날의 comprehensive adj. 종합적인 viewership n. 시청률 criticize v. 비판하다 favor v. 장려하다, 호의를 보이다 commercial adj. 상업적인 artistic adj. 예술적인 nomination n. 수상 후보

1. 특정세부사항 What   정답 (c)

해석 그래미 시상식이 처음 제정되었을 때 목적은 무엇이었는가?

(a) 특정 장르의 음악을 홍보하기 위해
(b) 음악의 커지는 인기로 돈을 벌기 위해
(c) 배후에서 일하는 인물들을 표창하기 위해
(d) 상위의 음악 중역들에게 상을 주기 위해

해설 1단락의 'American music executives created it to acknowledge ~ the other professionals who work behind the scenes.'에서 배후에서 일하는 다른 전문가들도 인정해주기 위해 미국의 음악계 중역들이 그래미 시상식을 제정했다고 했다. 따라서 (c)가 정답이다.

2. 특정세부사항 What   정답 (a)

해석 지문에 따르면, 수년간 그래미 시상식에 대해 무엇이 변했는가?

(a) 시상되는 상의 개수
(b) 수상자들이 받는 트로피의 종류
(c) 텔레비전 방송의 길이
(d) 시상식을 방송하는 방송망

해설 2단락의 'a total of 28 prizes given out. That number has fluctuated over the years as new genres and categories have emerged'에서 총 28개의 상이 시상되었고 이 숫자는 새로운 장르와 카테고리가 등장하면서 수년간 변동을 거듭했다고 했다. 따라서 (a)가 정답이다.

3. Not/True True 문제   정답 (b)

해석 그래미상 선정 과정에 대해 사실인 것은?

(a) 예술가들은 자격을 갖추려면 정해진 수의 곡을 발매해야 한다.
(b) 심사위원들은 그들이 심사하는 카테고리에서 전문가여야 한다.
(c) 후보작들은 네 개가 넘는 카테고리에서 나올 수 없다.
(d) 투표 수는 회원의 위원에 의해 집계되어야 한다.

해설 3단락의 'voting members ~ only judge ~ in categories in which they have expertise'에서 투표하는 회원들은 오직 자신이 전문 지식을 가진 카테고리에서만 심사한다고 했다. 따라서 (b)가 정답이다.

4. 특정세부사항 What   정답 (d)

해석 1990년대에, 레코딩 아카데미는 무엇을 했는가?

(a) 다양한 언어로 방송되었음
(b) 트로피의 디자인을 바꾸었음

(c) 후보작의 수를 늘렸음
(d) 새로운 유형의 그래미상을 도입했음

해설 4단락의 'Since 1997, the Recording Academy has also held a ~ Latin Grammys event to recognize recordings in Spanish and Portuguese.'에서 1997년 이래로 레코딩 아카데미는 스페인어와 포르투갈어로 발매되는 음반도 표창하기 위해 라틴 그래미 시상식도 개최해왔다고 했다. 따라서 (d)가 정답이다.

5. 추론 특정사실   정답 (b)

해석 그래미 시상식의 인기 하락의 원인은 무엇일 수 있는가?

(a) 음반 회사가 그것에 돈을 덜 쓰고 있다.
(b) 상이 재능보다 매출을 더 가치 있게 여긴다.
(c) 그래미상에서의 인정은 더 이상 가치가 없다.
(d) 카테고리가 음악에서의 최근 변화를 반영하지 못한다.

해설 5단락의 'Many criticize it for favoring commercial achievement rather than artistic ability.'에서 많은 사람들은 예술적 능력보다 오히려 상업적 성과를 장려한다고 그래미 시상식을 비판한다고 한 것을 통해, 상이 재능보다 매출을 더 가치 있게 여겨서 인기가 하락했음을 추론할 수 있다. 따라서 (b)가 정답이다.

6. 어휘 유의어   정답 (d)

해석 지문의 문맥에서, 'contributions'는 –을 의미한다.

(a) 양
(b) 기부
(c) 개선
(d) 공적

해설 3단락의 'individuals who have made ~ contributions.'는 '공헌'을 한 개인이라는 뜻이므로, '공적'이라는 비슷한 의미의 (d)가 정답이다.

7. 어휘 유의어   정답 (c)

해석 지문의 문맥에서, 'aptly'는 –을 의미한다.

(a) 충분히
(b) 완벽하게
(c) 적절히
(d) 공식적으로

해설 4단락의 'statue aptly shaped like a gramophone'은 축음기 모양으로 '적절히' 만들어진 조각상이라는 뜻이므로, '적절히'라는 같은 의미의 (c)가 정답이다.

지문의 내용을 올바르게 paraphrasing한 것을 고르세요.

01

> The cocktail party effect describes the brain's ability to segregate auditory streams and focus on one sound out of many. It helps explain how people at a crowded party will hear their names called out despite multiple voices competing for their attention.

(a) The cocktail party effect allows the brain to collect information from multiple sources.
(b) The cocktail party effect describes a phenomenon that occurs at large gatherings.

02

> Machu Picchu's construction was likely determined by particular features of the site's geography. Its high elevation and steep terrain forced builders to avoid transporting materials in and to use mostly locally found materials. Frequent earthquakes also required that building stones be cut and joined without concrete.

(a) Machu Picchu had to be built in a specific way because of its challenging location.
(b) Machu Picchu was built to take advantage of local building materials and techniques.

03

> Recently, some academics have disputed the Russell Group's long-standing claim to represent the UK's best public research universities. They say dozens of other organizations perform better and that its esteemed position is currently based more on marketing than on evidence.

(a) Some academics argue that the Russell Group's reputation is no longer supported by evidence.
(b) Some academics believe that the Russell Group needs to reform its marketing practices.

Vocabulary In the context of the passage, ☐ means _____ .

1 **segregate**	(a) collect	(b) differentiate	(c) disconnect	(d) prohibit
2 **transporting**	(a) shipping	(b) carrying	(c) storing	(d) removing
3 **esteemed**	(a) wealthy	(b) unique	(c) respected	(d) appreciative

지문을 읽고 문제에 알맞은 답을 고르세요.

AIR FORCE ONE

Air Force One is the name for airplanes in the United States Air Force that are used by the president for official travel. The name actually refers to a fleet of aircraft that have been manufactured and updated for presidential use since the 1950s.

Since the 1980s, the Air Force One fleet has consisted of two huge jumbo jets. Superficially, they are identical to the commercial aircraft that passengers fly on every day, albeit painted in distinctive colors. However, their spacious interiors have been converted to allow them to contain all of the facilities necessary to sustain US presidents as they travel. These include offices, conference rooms, sleeping berths, a medical room, and a kitchen that can feed up to 100 people.

The Air Force One planes are also equipped with advanced security features. Their information system allows for perfectly secure communications. The electronics onboard are designed to operate without interference, even from electromagnetic pulses. Furthermore, the airplanes' range is unlimited because they are capable of being refueled in flight without having to land. These qualities allow an Air Force One airplane to serve as a mobile command center to address any threats to the United States.

---

04 What does the term Air Force One actually refer to?

    (a) the aircraft that are used by US presidents

    (b) the Air Force fleet that protects the president from attack

05 Why most likely are jumbo jets used?

    (a) to make the plane difficult to distinguish from commercial aircraft

    (b) to give presidents enough space to carry out their duties

06 Which is one of the Air Force One planes' capabilities?

    (a) flying undetected by radar

    (b) receiving fuel while still in flight

Vocabulary In the context of the passage, ☐ means _____.

4 **converted**	(a) produced	(b) replaced	(c) adopted	(d) changed
5 **address**	(a) manage	(b) report	(c) prevent	(d) identify

UNIVERSAL STUDIOS

Universal Studios is a movie studio and theme park that began near Hollywood, California. It first opened in 1915 as Universal City, a place for tourists to learn about how films are made, and, since then, it has become a large entertainment brand with theme parks around the world.

The original park was sold in 1962, and the new management team expanded the tours and services to increase profits. The tours included stunt demonstrations staged for guests and access to the stars' dressing rooms. In addition, rides and a petting zoo were erected to help the park attract more children.

In 1968, however, the Screen Actors Guild complained of the disturbances caused by growing numbers of visitors to production areas where films were being made. The backlash from actors and production staff forced management to limit public access to certain areas.

Still, the success of the original Universal Studios led to expansion in other locations, such as Orlando, Florida. It was there that it truly became a theme park with many rides based on popular movies like *Jurassic Park* and *Harry Potter*.

07 According to the article, what is Universal Studios?

(a) a large chain of movie theaters
(b) a theme park and film studio

08 What helped the park become more interesting to children?

(a) fun rides and a zoo
(b) tours about animated films

09 Why were visitors prohibited from areas where films were being made?

(a) security concerns in the production areas
(b) an objection by an actors' organization

Vocabulary In the context of the passage, ☐ means _____ .

| 6 **staged** | (a) filmed | (b) hidden | (c) presented | (d) operated |
| 7 **backlash** | (a) response | (b) commentary | (c) announcement | (d) criticism |

BLUE-FOOTED BOOBY

The blue-footed booby is a seabird with brightly colored blue feet. It populates tropical regions along the periphery of the eastern Pacific from California down to Peru. It is one of six distinct species collectively known as boobies.

The bird's name is believed to come from the Spanish term *bobo*, meaning "stupid", because the tame birds had a reputation for landing aboard ships, apparently oblivious to hungry crew members who easily caught and ate them.

The blue-footed booby has a long bill, narrow and angular wings, and a brown-and-white, cigar-shaped body that varies in length from 65 to 85 centimeters, with the female being slightly larger than the male. A related species has red feet rather than blue, while another has a blue color on the face instead of the feet.

The blue-footed booby nests in large breeding colonies on exposed land areas. It hunts fish and squid by scanning for schools from high above the ocean and then plunging downward steeply to ambush their prey. Male boobies also display an elaborate courtship dance that involves alternately raising each foot and performing what ornithologists call sky pointing, or pointing their wings backward, raising their heads, and emitting a long whistle.

10 What is true about boobies?

(a) They became popular as pets among sailors.

(b) They displayed a seeming lack of intelligence.

11 How do female boobies differ from males?

(a) They tend to be bigger in size.

(b) They have blue faces instead of feet.

12 What do male boobies do during courtship?

(a) build nests on high clifftops

(b) whistle while doing a dance

정답·해석·해설 p.36

Vocabulary In the context of the passage, ☐ means _____.

Vocabulary 정답·해석 p.39

| 8 **periphery** | (a) line | (b) entrance | (c) boundary | (d) trail |
| 9 **ambush** | (a) stalk | (b) attack | (c) rescue | (d) scout |

1-7

PROSCIUTTO

Prosciutto is the generic term for an Italian dry-cured ham. <u>Characterized</u> by a sweet, delicate flavor, it is often served thinly sliced and raw in a style known as *prosciutto crudo*. The curing process makes the raw ham safe to eat. When it is served cooked, it is called *prosciutto cotto*.

The most famous prosciutto variety is Prosciutto di Parma PDO, which comes from the Emilia-Romagna region in Italy's north. The PDO designation stands for Protected Designation of Origin and signifies that the product is authentic and meets certain standards of quality.

Regardless of origin, all prosciuttos are made from the hind leg or thigh of an animal. In most cases, the animal is a pig or a wild boar. However, prosciutto may also be made using other animals, in which case the animal must be identified in the product's name, as in *prosciutto cotto d'agnello*, or lamb prosciutto.

To make prosciutto, the ham is first cleaned, salted, and left for two months. During this time, it is gradually pressed to drain all blood left in the meat. This must be done carefully to avoid breaking the bone. Next, the ham is washed and hung in a dark, well-ventilated environment. The surrounding air is important to the ham's final quality. It needs to be damp but cool to prevent spoilage. The duration of the drying process varies based on local climate and the ham's size. Once dry, it is placed on a hook to air, either at room temperature or in a temperature-controlled environment, for as long as 18 months. Some manufacturers cure the ham with sodium or potassium nitrites, which <u>increases</u> the quality of its salty flavor. Others use only sea salt.

Once sliced, prosciutto can be presented by itself or used to complement other dishes. In Italy, it is most commonly served as an antipasto, or appetizer, with cheese and other cured meats, or wrapped around pieces of fruit. Now eaten around the world, it is highly versatile and may also be added to pastas and salads, placed on pizza as a topping, or stuffed inside other meats.

1. How does *prosciutto cotto* differ from *prosciutto crudo*?

   (a) It is cured.
   (b) It is cooked.
   (c) It is moister.
   (d) It is cut into thick slices.

2. What is Italy's Emilia-Romagna region known for?

   (a) being the birthplace of *prosciutto crudo*
   (b) consuming the largest quantities of prosciutto
   (c) producing the best known variety of prosciutto
   (d) establishing standards for prosciutto production

3. What is similar about all varieties of prosciutto?

   (a) the time it takes to make
   (b) the kind of salt they contain
   (c) the part of the animal that is used
   (d) the age of the pigs they come from

4. Which is NOT a step in the process of making prosciutto?

   (a) washing in salt water
   (b) hanging in a darkened room
   (c) extracting blood from the meat
   (d) exposing to air for several months

5. Based on the article, why most likely is prosciutto consumed worldwide?

   (a) It is a representative dish of Italian cuisine.
   (b) It can be used as a topping for pizza.
   (c) It can be used in a wide variety of dishes.
   (d) It is the only form of dry-cured ham in the world.

6. In the context of the passage, Characterized means _____ .

   (a) Marked
   (b) Indicated
   (c) Typified
   (d) Symbolized

7. In the context of the passage, increases means _____ .

   (a) lowers
   (b) improves
   (c) recovers
   (d) solidifies

MANUL

The manul is a small wild cat inhabiting the grasslands and mountain steppes of Central Asia. It was first described as a new species in 1776 by the Prussian naturalist Peter Simon Pallas, which is why it is also named the Pallas's cat.

Including the tail, the manul is relatively small in <u>stature</u>, measuring about 65 to 91 cm long and weighing between 2.2 and 4.5 kg. It has a compact body, stubby legs, and dense coat of fur. The fur is a yellowish gray with dark markings that help the manul to blend with its surroundings. Unlike other small cats, the manul's pupils are round. It also has fewer teeth than is typical, with large canine teeth, and a flattened face with ears set low and wide apart.

Due to harsh conditions in its environment, the manul has a short breeding season. Females are pregnant for about two months before giving birth to up to six kittens. The large number of offspring is believed to make up for the fact that few of the kittens grow into adulthood. The kittens are born with a thick coat of fuzzy fur, which is replaced by an adult coat after two months. They begin hunting after four months and reach adult size after six months.

The manul is also notoriously difficult to spot. Apart from being solitary animals, males of the species move about a large area of about 98 km^2. The females largely live apart in a smaller area of about 23 km^2. Both mark their territories with scents. During the day, the manul spends most of its time in caves, crevices, or burrows before emerging in late afternoon to hunt. Lacking speed, it stalks and ambushes prey from behind the cover of low vegetation and rocky terrain. Its prey consists mostly of other small mammals.

Due to habitat degradation, a decline in prey numbers, and hunting, the manul is under threat of extinction. Attempts to <u>preserve</u> the species by breeding manuls in captivity have been generally unsuccessful. Although the manul breeds easily, it is vulnerable to infection from viruses that are not found in its usual habitat.

8. What is the article mainly about?

   (a) a domestic cat common in Prussia
   (b) a wild cat from Central Asia
   (c) a newly discovered cat species
   (d) an extinct species of cat

9. According to the passage, what distinguishes the manul from other small cats?

   (a) the color of its eyes
   (b) the shape of its pupils
   (c) the size of its claws
   (d) the roundness of its ears

10. Which is true about manul kittens?

   (a) They have a low survival rate.
   (b) They identify their parents by smell.
   (c) They start hunting at two months old.
   (d) They eat vegetation for the first six months.

11. Why is the manul most likely difficult to spot in its environment?

   (a) It is only active at night.
   (b) It mostly moves around alone.
   (c) It does not leave a scent behind.
   (d) It resembles other small mammals.

12. What is a challenge of raising the manul in captivity?

   (a) its vulnerability to unfamiliar diseases
   (b) its highly specific dietary requirements
   (c) its inability to live inside a cage
   (d) its preference for mating with a single partner

13. In the context of the passage, stature means _____.

   (a) size
   (b) quantity
   (c) capacity
   (d) importance

14. In the context of the passage, preserve means _____.

   (a) hide
   (b) store
   (c) freeze
   (d) protect

2주 말이 끝나는 해커스 지털프 독해 Level 2

DIVING

Diving is the sport of plunging into water from a platform or springboard, usually while performing acrobatics. Although diving contests were held in England in the 1800s, it was not until 1903 that it formally became a competitive sport. It was added to the Summer Olympic Games a year later.

The sport originated in Europe in the early 1800s. It allowed gymnasts to perform elaborate acrobatic feats without fear of injury from impact with the ground. Even today, gymnasts are particularly <u>disposed</u> to becoming professional divers, and many do. Both sports have similar requirements for strength, flexibility, and the ability to judge one's position while moving through the air.

In diving competitions, dives are performed from a 5- or 10-meter platform and a 1- or 3-meter springboard. Only the 10-meter dive and 3-meter dive are used in the Olympics. In either case, divers must complete 10 dives in sequence from a list they prepare and submit beforehand.

There are six main groups into which dives are classified: forward, backward, inward, reverse, twisting, and armstand. Each corresponds to the diver's position and orientation at the beginning of a dive, the direction the diver rotates during the descent, and whether the diver performs twists in the air. Armstand dives are only performed from a platform.

Judges rate divers based on how they accomplish each part of a dive, beginning with the takeoff or hurdle, then the flight or actual dive, and lastly the entry, or how the diver hits the water. The resulting score is multiplied by a degree of difficulty factor based on the number and combination of movements attempted.

At the highest levels of competition, degree of difficulty is less important than how a sequence of dives is arranged since divers all have about the same level of skill. The only way to gain an <u>edge</u> is to complete each dive as perfectly as possible. Consequently, divers adopt a strategy of organizing dives by level of personal comfort. This allows them to build up confidence and momentum as the competition progresses.

15. When did diving become an Olympic sport?

    (a) in the early 1900s
    (b) toward the end of the 1800s
    (c) during the 19th century
    (d) in the middle of the 1900s

16. According to the passage, why did diving initially appeal to gymnasts?

    (a) Gymnasiums were often built near pools.
    (b) Moving through water helped them build strength.
    (c) Their powerful leg muscles were suitable for diving.
    (d) Swimming pools provided a soft landing.

17. What must divers do when they participate in an Olympic competition?

    (a) register for membership in an organization
    (b) choose from one of two diving platforms
    (c) finish 10 dives from a list they hand in
    (d) complete at least one dive from every category

18. How are divers scored in competitive diving?

    (a) The divers' scores are determined by the number of movements and difficulty.
    (b) Divers are given a score that is divided by how many dives they did.
    (c) The judges give each diver a score out of 100.
    (d) Divers are scored based on the height of the board they jump from.

19. Why most likely do divers change their strategies for high-level competitions?

    (a) They need to impress judges with difficult dives.
    (b) They want to make the fewest mistakes possible.
    (c) They have to perform dives in quick succession.
    (d) They have fewer dives with which to earn a score.

20. In the context of the passage, disposed means _____.

    (a) biased
    (b) removed
    (c) inclined
    (d) arranged

21. In the context of the passage, edge means _____.

    (a) shape
    (b) border
    (c) ledge
    (d) advantage

NANDI

In Hindu mythology, Nandi is a guardian at the gates of Mount Kailash, the dwelling place of Shiva, one of Hinduism's principal deities. Traditionally portrayed as a white bull, Nandi also serves as Shiva's *vahana*, or his vehicle.

The word *Nandi* has its roots in the Tamil word *nandhu*, which means *to grow*, and the Sanskrit word *nandi*, which means *delight*. The worship of Shiva and Nandi is thought to have originated around the time that the Indus Valley Civilization flourished, between 3300 and 1200 BC. Multiple stone relics from that time, inscribed with the images of either Shiva or a bull, are cited as evidence of a long-standing tradition of Nandi worship. Nandi also appears on gold coins minted during the first and second centuries AD.

Accounts of Nandi's origins vary, but one story relates that he was the result of his father's strong desire for a child, expressed as worshipful pleas to Shiva. Impressed, Shiva granted Nandi as a blessing. However, Nandi was foretold to live a short life by Hindu sages and was prompted to seek Shiva's mercy. When Shiva appeared before him, Nandi innocently blurted out that he wished to be with Shiva forever. Shiva, having recently lost his bull, offered Nandi the role, and the two became permanent companions.

Some records describe Nandi in anthropomorphic form, with the head of a bull and four arms. His hands either gesture or grasp one of various objects such as a battle-axe or an official staff. Otherwise, Nandi is typically depicted as a seated bull.

Today, many Shiva temples from across India and Southeast Asia display large stone statues of a bull seated on a platform. The bull is usually in a position facing Shiva to show Nandi's eternal devotion to his master. To Hindu worshippers, this shows how devotees must focus on the creator of divine wisdom. Devotees decorate the bulls with bells, clappers, and floral garlands. In some Indian cities, tradition also dictates that live bulls dedicated to Shiva be permitted to roam the streets freely.

22. What is Nandi?

(a) a mythological bull
(b) a famous spiritual teacher
(c) a Hindu demon
(d) a stone guardian

23. According to the passage, what is the oldest evidence of Nandi worship?

(a) cave paintings
(b) ancient coins
(c) stone pieces
(d) antique documents

24. What does the story of Nandi's origins probably say about him?

(a) He is the child of Shiva.
(b) He was a farmer in life.
(c) He was made immortal.
(d) He was born with four arms.

25. How is Nandi's position in Shiva temples understood by Hindu devotees?

(a) It shows that they must create statues of Nandi.
(b) It shows that they must concentrate on the source of divine knowledge.
(c) It shows that they must thank Shiva for creating Nandi.
(d) It shows that they can enjoy immortality by worshipping Shiva.

26. Which of the following is NOT a tradition associated with Nandi?

(a) building bull statues in temples
(b) allowing bulls to roam city streets
(c) placing flowers on stone bulls
(d) sacrificing bulls at religious festivals

27. In the context of the passage, inscribed means _____.

(a) drawn
(b) carved
(c) painted
(d) colored

28. In the context of the passage, typically means _____.

(a) carefully
(b) practically
(c) usually
(d) successfully

BERLIN WALL

The Berlin Wall was a physical barrier that separated West Berlin not just from East Berlin but also from the rest of Germany from 1961 to 1989. It became a symbol of the Cold War ideological divide that emerged after World War II between the politically liberal countries of Western Europe and the communist Eastern Bloc.

Following their defeat of the Nazis in World War II, the four Allied powers of the United States, the United Kingdom, France, and the Soviet Union divided Germany into four zones. The capital city of Berlin, despite being located within the Soviet zone, was further subdivided and became the seat of Allied control. Shortly thereafter, serious disagreements arose between the Soviets and their allies, prompting the Soviets to gradually tighten their control over East Germany. For instance, they nationalized industries, imposed severe punishments on people who opposed Communist Party directives, and introduced mandatory schooling in Marxist-Leninist thought.

Hoping to escape Soviet oppression, over 2.5 million East Germans fled to West Germany between 1949 and 1961, and the wall was built as a direct response to this mass departure. Although presented as a way to protect East Germans from Western influence, the wall was actually intended to stop the flow of numerous skilled workers, professionals, and intellectuals to the West.

What began as a simple wall of barbed wire and cement blocks eventually was replaced by five-meter-high barriers defended by armed guards, electrified fences, and fortifications. By the 1980s, it extended 45 km through Berlin's center and a further 120 km around West Berlin, isolating the city within East Germany.

It was not until October of 1989 that the wall came down, after East Germany's leadership was overthrown due to the political revolution that swept across the Eastern Bloc and removed the communist rulers. By this time, of the roughly 100,000 who attempted the perilous crossing into West Germany, around 5,000 had succeeded and around 200 had been killed. Both East and West Germans celebrated the Berlin Wall's collapse. Demolition officially began the next year and ended in 1992.

29. What is true about the Berlin Wall?

    (a) It was not completed until 1989.
    (b) It was built jointly by several countries.
    (c) It became a symbol of political
        differences.
    (d) It triggered the start of the Cold War.

30. How did the Soviet Union attempt to gain
    greater influence over the East Germans?

    (a) by providing financial incentives
    (b) by introducing a new constitution
    (c) through frequent cultural exchanges
    (d) through forced programs of education

31. What most likely caused people to leave
    East Germany between 1949 and 1961?

    (a) growing signs that the Berlin Wall
        would be built
    (b) the lure of easy money to be made in
        the West
    (c) increasing restrictions on personal
        freedoms
    (d) influential media campaigns from the
        West

32. What happened by the early 1980s?

    (a) The wall became increasingly
        neglected.
    (b) West Germans began building tunnels
        beneath the wall.
    (c) The wall was lengthened to enclose a
        larger area.
    (d) East Germans began shooting at
        targets beyond the wall.

33. Based on the article, what ultimately led to
    the collapse of the Berlin Wall?

    (a) a revolution that brought down
        communist states
    (b) horror at the number of people killed at
        the wall
    (c) the high cost of maintaining the wall's
        defenses
    (d) activist movements on both sides of
        the wall

34. In the context of the passage, numerous
    means _____.

    (a) few
    (b) great
    (c) many
    (d) different

35. In the context of the passage, perilous
    means _____.

    (a) risky
    (b) delicate
    (c) rugged
    (d) insecure

정답·해석·해설 p.39

PART 3에서 선별한 다음의 지텔프 빈출 어휘들을 암기한 후 퀴즈로 확인해보세요.

fluctuate v. 변동을 거듭하다		**access** n. 입장, 접근	
emerge v. 등장하다, 나오다		**backlash** n. 반발	
field n. 분야		**concern** n. 문제, 걱정	
technical adj. 기술적인		**distinct** adj. 뚜렷이 다른, 별개의	
aspect n. 측면, 양상		**aboard** adj. (배·비행기 등에) 탄, 탑승한	
criticize v. 비판하다		**steeply** adv. 가파르게	
favor v. 장려하다, 호의를 보이다		**alternately** adv. 번갈아, 교대로	
construction n. 건축 양식		**delicate** adj. 은은한, 연약한	
geography n. 지형		**signify** v. 의미하다, 나타내다	
academic n. 학자		**authentic** adj. 진품인	
dispute v. 반박하다		**moist** adj. 촉촉한	
identical adj. 동일한, 똑같은		**cuisine** n. 음식, 요리	
distinctive adj. 뚜렷이 구별되는		**inhabit** v. 서식하다, 살다	
convert v. 변형하다		**stature** n. 크기	
advanced adj. 상급의		**compact** adj. 작은, 소형의	
profit n. 수익		**dense** adj. 촘촘한	
demonstration n. 시범, 설명		**harsh** adj. 혹독한	

Quiz 각 단어의 알맞은 뜻을 찾아 연결하세요.

01 field	ⓐ 뚜렷이 구별되는	06 criticize	ⓗ 촘촘한
	ⓑ 은은한, 연약한		ⓘ 변동을 거듭하다
02 distinctive	ⓒ 반박하다	07 aspect	ⓙ 지형
03 profit	ⓓ 분야	08 fluctuate	ⓚ 측면, 양상
	ⓔ 크기		ⓛ 서식하다, 살다
04 delicate	ⓕ 변형하다	09 cuisine	ⓜ 음식, 요리
05 stature	ⓖ 수익	10 geography	ⓝ 비판하다

정답 ⓕ 10 ⓙ 09 ⓘ 08 ⓚ 07 ⓝ 06 ⓔ 05 ⓑ 04 ⓖ 03 ⓐ 02 ⓓ 01

pregnant adj. 임신한

offspring n. 새끼, 자식

solitary adj. 단독 생활을 하는

territory n. 영역, 지역

mammal n. 포유동물

domestic adj. 집안의, 가정의

dietary adj. 식이의

elaborate adj. 정교한

dispose v. 생각이 들게 하다, 경향을 갖게 하다

strength n. 힘

judge v. 판단하다, 심사위원을 하다 n. 심사위원

submit v. 제출하다

correspond v. 해당하다

strategy n. 전략

dwell v. 살다, 거주하다

portray v. 묘사하다

vehicle n. 탈 것

worship n. 숭배

flourish v. 번창하다

relic n. 유물

evidence n. 증거

account n. 이야기, 계좌

grant v. 주다, 응하다

permanent adj. 영원한

eternal adj. 영원한

physical adj. 물리적인

barrier n. 장벽

liberal adj. 진보주의의

defeat n. 타도, 패배

impose v. 처벌하다

mandatory adj. 의무의

overthrow v. 타도하다

collapse n. 붕괴

incentive n. 장려금

Quiz 각 단어의 알맞은 뜻을 찾아 연결하세요.

01 flourish	ⓐ 전략	06 offspring	ⓗ 붕괴
	ⓑ 정교한		ⓘ 새끼, 자식
02 elaborate	ⓒ 물리적인	07 relic	ⓙ 영원한
03 physical	ⓓ 해당하다	08 collapse	ⓚ 증거
04 correspond	ⓔ 의무의	09 dietary	ⓛ 영역, 지역
	ⓕ 포유동물		ⓜ 유물
05 mammal	ⓖ 번창하다	10 territory	ⓝ 식이의

정답 01 ⓖ 02 ⓑ 03 ⓒ 04 ⓓ 05 ⓕ 06 ⓘ 07 ⓜ 08 ⓗ 09 ⓝ 10 ⓛ

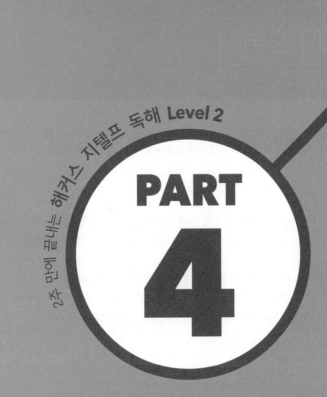

PART 4

비즈니스 편지

Business Letter

PART 4 비즈니스 편지 Business Letter

PART 4에서는 업무를 요청하거나, 서비스를 홍보하는 등의 비즈니스 편지 지문이 출제된다. 4개 파트 중에서 유일하게 제목이 없는 지문 유형이며, 편지의 주제나 목적, 지문에서 언급된 세부적인 내용을 묻는 문제가 다양하게 출제된다.

🔵 출제 토픽

주로 업무 제안 및 요청, 고객 서비스, 인사 및 입학 관련 편지가 골고루 출제된다. 기존에는 사업을 제안하는 내용이 많았지만, 최근에는 고객의 컴플레인 혹은 감사 관련 내용이 상대적으로 많이 출제되고 있다.

· 제안/요청	행사 발표자로 초대, 서류 작성 요청, 제품 구매 제안, 자선 행사 파트너 제안
· 고객 서비스	레스토랑 서비스 컴플레인, 아이를 찾아준 직원에게 감사 인사, 새로운 지점 개업 안내, 서비스 홍보
· 인사/입학	입사 지원, 일자리 제의, 일자리 제의 수락, 퇴사 의사 전달, 대학원 합격 통보

🔵 문제 유형

유일하게 목적 문제가 출제되는 파트이며, 주로 첫 문제로 등장한다. 간혹 편지의 주제나 수신인 혹은 발신인이 다음에 할 일을 묻는 문제가 출제되기도 한다.

주제/목적	편지의 목적을 묻는다. **Why** did Mr. Stuart **write** a letter to Ms. Kim? Mr. Stuart는 왜 Ms. Kim에게 편지를 썼는가?
특정세부사항	요청하는 것, 제공하는 서비스, 행사 안내, 채용 과정 등 지문에서 언급된 세부사항을 묻는다. **How** will the event benefit the attendees? 행사는 참가자들에게 어떻게 도움이 될 것인가?
Not/True	편지에 작성되어 있는 것에 대해 사실이거나 사실이 아닌 것을 묻는다. What is **true** about a product with a 30% discount? 30퍼센트 할인이 되는 제품에 대해 사실인 것은?
추론	편지의 내용을 통해 추론할 수 있는 것을 묻는다. What should Pitt **probably** do to receive the product? 제품을 받기 위해 Pitt는 무엇을 해야 할 것 같은가?
어휘	지문의 문맥에서 밑줄 어휘의 유의어가 무엇인지를 묻는다. In the context of the passage, considerable means _____. 지문의 문맥에서, 'considerable'은 ~을 의미한다.

🔵 핵심 전략

1. '편지의 목적 → 요청 사항 및 답변 → 세부 설명 → 끝인사'의 패턴화된 흐름에서 출제되는 빈출 문제들을 알아두어야 한다.

2. 목적, 요청 사항, 당부하는 내용은 관련 표현을 익혀두면 쉽게 찾을 수 있다.

3. 수신인과 발신인의 정보를 파악해두면 두 사람의 관계, 소속 등을 알 수 있어 세부적인 내용을 이해할 때 도움이 된다.

지문 흐름	흐름에 따른 빈출 문제

Chloe McLain
108 Maple가
앨버타 주, 에드먼턴

Chloe McLain께,

저희 두리하나 마켓에서 주문해주셔서 감사드립니다. 정말 죄송합니다만, 5월 27일 주문하신 제품 중 초록색 블라우스의 갑작스러운 주문 증가로 인해 당일 출고가 정상적으로 이뤄지지 못하고 있습니다. 기존 수령 예정일보다 일주일에서 열흘 정도 배송이 늦어질 것으로 예상됩니다.

저희의 불찰로 인해 이러한 불편함을 끼쳐 정말 죄송합니다. 그 대신, 주문하신 상품에 대해 지불하신 배송비는 무료 처리해드리겠으며, 이는 적립 포인트로 환급해드릴 예정입니다. 더불어, 두리하나 마켓에서 사용하실 수 있는 10% 할인 쿠폰도 고객님께 지급해드리겠습니다. 이로써 저희가 끼친 불편이 조금이라도 덜어지기를 바랍니다.

할인 쿠폰은 고객님의 계정으로 자동 지급될 예정이므로, 사이트에 로그인하시면 마이페이지의 쿠폰 탭에서 확인이 가능하실 것입니다. 쿠폰은 20달러 이상 구매 시 사용 가능하며, 중복 할인도 가능하지만, 배송비를 제외한 금액에 대한 할인이 적용되는 점 유의해주시기 바랍니다.

관련하여 문의하실 사항이 있으시다면, cservice@twoone.com으로 메일을 보내시거나, 555-7654로 전화해주세요.

Lauren Murphy 드림
고객서비스 센터
두리하나 마켓

수신인 정보

편지의 목적 및 배경 설명

편지의 목적을 묻는 문제가 출제된다.
[ex] Why did Ms. Murphy write a letter to Ms. McLain?
Ms. Murphy는 왜 Ms. McLain에게 편지를 썼는가?

문제가 무엇인지 묻는 문제가 출제된다.
[ex] Why is Ms. Murphy having a problem with delivering the products?
Ms. Murphy는 왜 물품을 배송하는 것에 문제를 겪고 있는가?

문제에 대한 해결책

안내 사항 등에 대한 세부적인 것을 묻는 문제가 출제된다.
[ex] What will Ms. McLain get as compensation?
Ms. McLain은 보상으로 무엇을 받을 것인가?
[ex] How will the discount coupon be delivered?
할인 쿠폰은 어떻게 전달될 것인가?

내용 부가 설명

부가 설명에서 언급된 세부적인 것을 묻는 문제가 출제된다.
[ex] What is not true about the coupon?
쿠폰에 대해 사실이 아닌 것은?
[ex] What will Chloe McLain find in her Mypage?
Chloe McLain은 마이페이지에서 무엇을 확인할 수 있을 것인가?

끝인사

수신인이 무엇을 할 수 있는지를 묻는 문제가 출제된다.
[ex] What will Chloe McLain do if she has an inquiry?
Chloe McLain이 문의 사항이 생길 시 무엇을 할 것인가?

발신인 정보

1. 편지의 목적

① **I'm writing to** ~하기 위해 편지를 씁니다
I'm writing to apply for the position you have advertised on your website.
당신이 웹사이트에 광고한 직무에 지원하기 위해 편지를 씁니다.

② **I'm pleased to** ~하게 되어 기쁩니다
I'm pleased to invite you to be our keynote speaker.
저희의 기조연설자로 귀하를 초대하게 되어 기쁩니다.

2. 요청 사항

③ **Could you ~?** ~해 주실 수 있으십니까?
Could you send me your registration number?
당신의 등록 번호를 제게 보내주실 수 있으십니까?

④ **Be sure to** 반드시 ~해 주세요
Be sure to visit our website to see the rest of our new products.
나머지 저희 신제품을 확인하기 위해 반드시 저희 웹사이트를 방문해주세요.

3. 당부

⑤ **don't hesitate to** 망설이지 말고 ~해 주세요
Should you have any concerns, **don't hesitate to** contact us at cservice@twoone.com.
용무가 있으시다면, 망설이지 말고 cservice@twoone.com으로 연락해주세요.

⑥ **Please feel free to** 편하게 ~해주세요
Please feel free to call me at 754-3288.
754-3288로 편하게 연락해주세요.

1. 제안/요청

inform v. 알리다, 통지하다	**remind** v. 다시 한번 알려주다, 상기시키다
host v. (행사를) 주최하다 n. 주최 측	**require** v. 요구하다, 필요하다
instruct v. 지시하다, 가르치다	**charge** v. 청구하다 n. 요금
publish v. 출판하다, 게재하다	**financial** adj. 금융의
depend on phr. 의존하다, 믿다	**budget** n. 예산, 비용
deadline n. 기한, 마감 일자	**cause** n. 원인, 이유 v. 야기하다
avoid v. 피하다, 모면하다	**permit** v. 허용하다 n. 허가증

2. 고객 서비스

branch n. 지점, 분점	**appreciate** v. 고마워하다, 인정하다
annual adj. 연례의	**commercial** adj. 상업의
loyal adj. 충실한, 성실한	**complain** v. 불평하다, 항의하다
discount n. 할인	**apologize** v. 사과하다
bargain n. 싸게 사는 물건, 흥정	**facility** n. 시설, 기능
detail n. 세부 사항	**guarantee** v. 보장하다 n. 품질 보증서
brochure n. (광고용) 책자	**stock** n. 재고품, 재고

3. 인사/채용

employ v. 고용하다	**volunteer** v. 자진하다 n. 자원봉사자
engage v. 고용하다, 사로잡다	**contract** v. 계약하다 n. 계약서
apply v. 지원하다, 적용하다	**fulfill** v. 완수하다, 지키다
recruitment n. 신규 모집, 채용	**boost** v. 신장시키다, 북돋우다
department n. 부서	**circumstance** n. 환경, 상황
formal adj. 공식적인, 정식의	**necessary** n. 필요한, 불가피한
opportunity n. 기회	**reference** n. 참고, 추천서
entitle v. 자격을 주다	**assign** v. 배정하다, 맡기다

May 21, 2022

Mr. Francis Morales
Senior Vice President
Armor Investment

Dear Mr. Morales:

1번 키워드

1 In connection with our discussion during last month's gathering of the Purcell Commerce Club, **I am writing to formally propose a technical partnership between our two firms**.

2번 키워드

2 You raised the issue of **Armor's challenges in keeping its services up-to-date with the ever-changing financial rules** of the different states in which it operates. We can help you facilitate this process by developing a system for conveying regulatory updates from the head office to your offices nationwide.

3 **The project will require a significant investment of time and money.** The engineers who will execute the project have extensive backgrounds in program development. **However, Hartsoft itself is still relatively young and small**. Therefore, we propose **a partnership in which Armor funds research and development using Hartsoft personnel.**

3번 키워드

4번 키워드

4 **This approach will remove the need for Armor to recruit its own team.** We are prepared to supervise all stages of development including implementation and training.

5번 키워드

5 Please review the **enclosed documents for details, including conditions for the ownership of the final program.**

Sincerely,

Kathleen Hart
President and CEO
Hartsoft Innovation

지문 흐름

수신인 정보

편지의 목적

배경 설명 및
제휴 제안

서비스
세부 내용

서비스 장점

끝인사

발신인 정보

편지의 목적을 묻고 있으므로, 1단락에서 단서를 찾는다.

1. Why did Kathleen Hart write to Francis Morales?

   (a) to review suggestions from a meeting
   (b) to discuss plans for a future event
   (c) to suggest a business collaboration
   (d) to promote a commerce club

Armor 보험사는 무슨 어려움을 겪었는지 묻고 있으므로, 질문의 키워드 difficulty가 challenges로 paraphrasing되어 언급된 2단락에서 단서를 찾는다.

2. According to the letter, what did Armor Investment have difficulty with?

   (a) its recent changes in personnel
   (b) its response to rule changes
   (c) its expansion of services
   (d) its database of client requests

왜 회사의 연혁과 크기를 논했던 것 같은지를 묻고 있으므로, 질문의 키워드 age and size가 young and small로 paraphrasing되어 언급된 3단락에서 단서를 찾는다.

3. Why most likely did Kathleen Hart discuss the age and size of her business?

   (a) to provide assurances about its capabilities
   (b) to explain the reason behind its success
   (c) to demonstrate its suitability as a partner
   (d) to illustrate why it requires financial backing

Hartsoft 사가 하겠다고 제안하는 것이 아닌 것을 묻고 있으므로, Hartsoft 사가 제공하는 서비스에 대한 세부 내용 및 장점이 언급된 3단락과 4단락에서 단서를 찾는다.

4. What is NOT something that Hartsoft suggests they will do?

   (a) build a system for revising services
   (b) help Armor recruit its own team
   (c) provide Hartsoft's engineers for a project
   (d) oversee development and training

동봉된 서류에 어떤 세부 사항이 포함되어 있는지를 묻고 있으므로, 질문의 키워드 enclosed documentation이 enclosed documents로 언급된 5단락에서 단서를 찾는다.

5. What details are included in the enclosed documentation?

   (a) terms regarding control of a program
   (b) conditions for the sale of a company
   (c) procedures for resolving disputes
   (d) arrangements for an upcoming meeting

6. In the context of the passage, raised means _____.

   (a) dismissed
   (b) lifted
   (c) mentioned
   (d) increased

7. In the context of the passage, execute means _____.

   (a) succeed
   (b) carry
   (c) do
   (d) train

해석 및 해설 뒷장에서 확인하기 ➡

2022년 5월 21일

Mr. Francis Morales
수석 부사장
Armor 투자사

Mr. Morales께:

1 지난달 Purcell 상공회 모임에서 저희가 논의했던 것에 이어, [1]저희 두 회사 간 기술 제휴를 공식적으로 제안하기 위해 편지를 씁니다.

2 당신은 각각 다른 주들에서 운영되는 [2]변화무쌍한 금융 규정 때문에 서비스를 최신으로 유지하는 데 Armor 사가 겪고 있는 어려움에 대한 사안을 언급했습니다. 저희는 본사로부터 전국에 있는 귀사의 지사에 규제 업데이트를 전달하는 [4(a)]시스템을 개발함으로써 이 과정을 용이하게 하는 데 도움을 드릴 수 있습니다.

3 [3]이 프로젝트는 상당한 시간과 돈의 투자를 필요로 할 것입니다. 이 프로젝트를 수행할 엔지니어들은 프로그램 개발에 관해 광범위한 배경지식을 갖고 있습니다. [3]하지만, Hartsoft 사 자체는 아직 상대적으로 젊고 작습니다. 그러므로, 저희는 [4(b)(c)]Armor 사가 Hartsoft 사의 인적 자원을 활용한 연구 개발에 자금을 대는 제휴를 제안합니다.

4 [4(b)]이 방법은 Armor 사가 자체 팀을 위해 인력을 채용할 필요가 없게 할 것입니다. [4(d)]저희는 시행과 교육을 포함한 모든 개발 단계를 감독할 준비가 되어 있습니다.

5 [5]최종 프로그램의 소유권에 대한 조건을 포함하는 세부 사항은 동봉된 서류를 확인해주시기 바랍니다.

Kathleen Hart 드림
회장 및 최고 경영자
Hartsoft 이노베이션

어휘 **gathering** n. 모임 **formally** adv. 공식적으로 **propose** v. 제안하다 **partnership** n. 제휴 **firm** n. 회사, 기업 **issue** n. 사안, 문제 **challenge** n. 어려움, 고난 **up-to-date** adj. 최신의 **ever-changing** adj. 변화무쌍한 **facilitate** v. 용이하게 하다 **convey** v. 전달하다 **nationwide** adj. 전국적인 **investment** n. 투자 **execute** v. 수행하다 **extensive** adj. 광범위한 **fund** v. 자금을 대다; n. 자금 **personnel** n. 인적 자원, 직원 **approach** n. 방법, 접근법 **recruit** v. 채용하다 **supervise** v. 감독하다 **implementation** n. 시행 **enclosed** adj. 동봉된 **condition** n. 조건, 상태 **ownership** n. 소유권

1. 주제/목적 편지의 목적   정답 (c)

해석 왜 Kathleen Hart는 Francis Morales에게 편지를 썼는가?

(a) 회의에서의 제안에 대해 검토하기 위해
(b) 향후의 행사를 위한 계획을 논의하기 위해
(c) 사업 제휴를 제안하기 위해
(d) 상공회를 홍보하기 위해

해석 1단락의 'I am writing to formally propose a technical partnership between our two firms'에서 두 회사 간 기술 제휴를 공식적으로 제안하기 위해 편지를 쓴다고 했다. 따라서 (c)가 정답이다.

2. 특정세부사항 What   정답 (b)

해석 편지에 따르면, Armor 투자사는 무슨 어려움을 겪었는가?

(a) 인적 자원의 최근 변화
(b) 규정 변화에 대한 대응
(c) 서비스 확장
(d) 고객 요청의 데이터베이스

해석 2단락의 'Armor's challenges in keeping its services up-to-date with the ever-changing financial rules'에서 변화무쌍한 금융 규정 때문에 서비스를 최신으로 유지하는 데 Armor 사가 겪고 있는 어려움이라고 했다. 따라서 (b)가 정답이다.

3. 추론 특정사실   정답 (d)

해석 Kathleen Hart는 왜 자신의 회사의 연혁과 크기를 논했던 것 같은가?

(a) 역량에 대한 확신을 제공하기 위해
(b) 성공의 원인을 설명하기 위해
(c) 파트너로서의 적합성을 보여주기 위해
(d) 재정적 지원이 필요한 이유를 설명하기 위해

해석 3단락의 'The project will require a significant investment of time and money.'에서 이 프로젝트는 상당한 시간과 돈의 투자를 필요로 할 것이라고 한 뒤, 'However, Hartsoft itself is still relatively young and small.'에서 하지만 Hartsoft 사 자체는 아직 상대적으로 젊고 작다고 한 것을 통해, 재정적 지원이 필요한 이유를 설명하기 위해 회사의 연혁과 크기를 논했던 것임을 추론할 수 있다. 따라서 (d)가 정답이다.

4. Not/True Not 문제   정답 (b)

해석 Hartsoft 사가 하겠다고 제안하는 것이 아닌 것은?

(a) 서비스를 변경하기 위한 시스템을 구축함
(b) Armor 사가 자체 팀을 채용하는 것을 도움
(c) 프로젝트를 위해 Hartsoft 사의 엔지니어를 제공함
(d) 개발 및 교육을 감독함

해석 3단락의 'a partnership in which Armor funds research and development using Hartsoft personnel'에서 Armor 사가 Hartsoft 사의 인적 자원을 활용한 연구 개발에 자금을 대는 제휴를 언급한 뒤, 4단락의 'This approach will remove the need for Armor to recruit its own team.'에서 이 방법은 Armor 사가 자체 팀을 위해 인력을 채용할 필요가 없게 할 것이라고 했다. 따라서 (b)가 정답이다. (a)는 2단락, (c)는 3단락, (d)는 4단락에서 언급되었다.

5. 특정세부사항 What   정답 (a)

해석 동봉된 서류에는 어떤 세부 사항이 포함되어 있는가?

(a) 프로그램의 지배권과 관련된 조항
(b) 회사 매매를 위한 조건
(c) 분쟁을 해결하기 위한 절차
(d) 다가오는 회의를 위한 계획

해석 5단락의 'enclosed documents for details, including conditions for the ownership of the final program'에서 최종 프로그램의 소유권의 조건을 포함하는 동봉된 서류라고 했다. 따라서 (a)가 정답이다.

6. 어휘 유의어   정답 (c)

해석 지문의 문맥에서, 'raised'는 -을 의미한다.

(a) 해산시켰다
(b) 들어올렸다
(c) 언급했다
(d) 증가시켰다

해석 2단락의 'You raised the issue'는 사안을 '언급했다'는 뜻이므로, '언급했다'라는 같은 의미의 (c)가 정답이다.

7. 어휘 유의어   정답 (c)

해석 지문의 문맥에서, 'execute'는 -을 의미한다.

(a) 성공하다
(b) 나르다
(c) 하다
(d) 교육하다

해석 3단락의 'The engineers who will execute the project'는 프로젝트를 '수행할' 엔지니어들이라는 뜻이므로, '하다'라는 비슷한 의미의 (c)가 정답이다.

지문의 내용을 올바르게 paraphrasing한 것을 고르세요.

01

> We are writing today because you expressed an interest in one of Hanson Industries' products, namely the EJ-800 product sorter. The EJ-800 is perfectly adapted to your production needs and will improve efficiency at your manufacturing plant by 40 percent.

(a) Hanson Industries is interested in using the EJ-800 to improve its manufacturing process.

(b) Hanson Industries is selling a product called the EJ-800 to manufacturing firms.

02

> The Civic Action Committee invites Mason Sports to participate in our 6th Annual Charity Fair as a sponsor. Your assistance will help us make this event a memorable one. The event will help equip local youth groups with sports gear.

(a) A community organization is seeking funding assistance for a charity event.

(b) Local businesses are holding an annual sports fair for local youth groups.

03

> I can inform you that KPCI's executive team has chosen to adopt the terms outlined in Farsi International's last merger proposal and recommended no further changes. However, the final agreement still has to be approved by KPCI's board of directors.

(a) KPCI is close to reaching a final merger agreement with Farsi International.

(b) KPCI has obtained approval for a merger from its shareholders and board of directors.

Vocabulary In the context of the passage, ☐ means _____ .

1 **adapted**	(a) improved	(b) identified	(c) outlined	(d) suited
2 **equip**	(a) recommend	(b) prepare	(c) provide	(d) submit
3 **adopt**	(a) accept	(b) enclose	(c) borrow	(d) introduce

지문을 읽고 문제에 알맞은 답을 고르세요.

Insurance Solutions

Dear Mr. Jacobs:

I am writing to make a complaint about the service I received from your firm following my recent car accident. I have never experienced such a difficult claims procedure or such habitually rude staff.

As you know, on the 3rd of March a truck collided with my car on a junction of Highway 112. My car's black box showed that no blame could be attributed to me. Indeed, the truck driver admitted his brakes had failed. My injuries confined me to a hospital bed for two weeks.

I contacted your firm and was rudely informed that my case was difficult. When I was referred to you, you told me that the claim was delayed as your firm could not determine who was responsible, as my car was old and, according to you, had not been adequately maintained. I was then interrogated by one of your associates, who had clearly been ordered to make me accept blame for the crash.

Considering these circumstances, I believe compensation is in order, so I am consulting with my lawyer to plan legal action against your firm. I await your reply.

Sincerely,
William Morris

---

04 What is the purpose of Morris's letter?

(a) to ask for a refund on his insurance contract
(b) to criticize the process of receiving his claim

05 According to Morris, why did a truck driver crash into his car?

(a) The truck driver was driving too fast.
(b) The truck suffered from brake failure.

06 How does Morris plan to get compensation from the company?

(a) by using a lawyer to take them to court
(b) by getting them to pay for repairs to his car

Vocabulary In the context of the passage, ☐ means _____ .

4 **habitually**	(a) patiently	(b) aggressively	(c) persistently	(d) willingly
5 **ordered**	(a) reprimanded	(b) commanded	(c) prohibited	(d) obeyed

September 15, 2021

Ken Murray
Accounting Manager
Technology P&I

Dear Mr. Murray:

I would like to notify you that I am resigning from my position in the company. I have been offered the post of senior accounting manager at another firm, and after careful consideration I have decided to accept it.

I want to thank you for all the support you have given me over the past few years. I have become very close with many staff members at Technology P&I, and I will miss working here very much.

However, I would like to highlight several issues that I have faced. Often, there is poor communication between divisions, leading to missed deadlines and incorrect contracts. Overall, there is a persistent lack of cooperation among departments. In addition, during the past year, my workload has increased dramatically as the company has taken on more clients. Although I was given more responsibilities and performed well, my pay has not increased.

Given these problems, I was unable to refuse this more senior role. As our company requires a two-week notice, I can continue working until September 30. Please let me know what you would like me to do to complete the transfer of my duties.

Sincerely,
Tom Phillips

07 Which is one cause of problems at the company?

(a) bad communication between teams
(b) a lack of departmental management

08 Based on the letter, what can probably be said about Tom Phillips's current company?

(a) It has been taken over in the past year.
(b) It has grown in the last year.

09 When will be Tom Phillips's last day of work?

(a) the 16th of September
(b) the last day of September

Vocabulary In the context of the passage, ☐ means _____ .

6 **close**	(a) aware	(b) friendly	(c) near	(d) distant
7 **performed**	(a) did	(b) acted	(c) behaved	(d) existed

December 12, 2021

Dear Ms. O'Connor,

I am pleased to tell you that you have been admitted into Bryson University's undergraduate degree program in medicine beginning in the fall of next year. Congratulations on this remarkable milestone.

The school's medical program is highly competitive and receives applications from thousands of students each year. We take great care to select only the most highly qualified candidates based on academic performance, extracurricular activities, and demonstrations of personal character. Your acceptance therefore indicates that we are confident you have the potential to succeed here as a student.

In March of next year, you will receive an invitation to participate in a three-day event on campus. It includes a guided tour of the grounds, social gatherings with current and former students, and the opportunity to sit in on a class of your choosing.

If you need help with other aspects of the admissions process, including securing financial assistance or student housing, please feel free to contact us. We offer generous aid to help students shoulder the many costs of a college education. You can find information on this and more on our website, www.brysonu.edu.

Sincerely,

Adam Roose
Dean of Admissions
Bryson University

10 Why is Mr. Roose writing to Ms. O'Connor?

(a) to congratulate her that she earned a medical degree
(b) to inform her that she has been accepted into college

12 Which is not part of the planned activities in March?

(a) a building inauguration
(b) a classroom observation

정답·해석·해설 p.50

11 According to the letter, what is true about Bryson University?

(a) It is interested in more than an applicant's grades.
(b) It welcomes financial contributions from former students.

Vocabulary In the context of the passage, [   ] means _____.   Vocabulary 정답·해석 p.53

| 8 **milestone** | (a) marker | (b) breakthrough | (c) occasion | (d) turnaround |
| 9 **shoulder** | (a) pay | (b) move | (c) lift | (d) bump |

1-7

Ms. Rebecca Hauser
Managing Editor
Carolinas Media

Dear Ms. Hauser:

I am writing to recommend Mr. Joel Medford for the editorial internship position at Carolinas Media. I have had the opportunity to observe Joel's progress over the past two years as his professor here at the Brady University Graduate School of Journalism and have been impressed by the qualities he has displayed.

First and foremost, Joel has the exact qualifications you are seeking. He is highly skilled at both research and writing, as is evident from the academic awards he <u>garnered</u> in our graduate course. In addition, he manages his time well and can be depended on to deliver work on deadline, which is something he has done both as a student and as a writer for the university's student paper.

Recently, I assisted Joel in developing his final dissertation, which was about social media and public attitudes. Through his analysis of social media's impact, he revealed the ways in which social platforms can be used to spread misinformation. In the paper, Joel presented a well-considered argument, which was backed up by a range of <u>titles</u> by relevant academics.

Apart from practical skills, Joel has also proven that he is a genuine and sympathetic person whose maturity has earned him the respect of his colleagues. In his short time at the university, he has shown a professional and conscientious attitude to his work.

Overall, I believe that Joel would make an excellent addition to your team, where he would be able to utilize his skills very effectively on your range of academic journals. If you have any questions, please feel free to contact me at 555-3209.

Sincerely,

Patrick Goode

Professor of Media Studies
Brady University Graduate School

1. Why did Patrick Goode write Rebecca Hauser a letter?

   (a) to commend a student for a job
   (b) to inquire about openings at a magazine
   (c) to grade her recent academic work
   (d) to describe her university course

2. According to Patrick Goode, which qualification does Joel Medford have?

   (a) He has years of experience.
   (b) He completed an internship.
   (c) He hands his work in on time.
   (d) He is skilled at social media.

3. What can most likely be said about Joel Medford's dissertation?

   (a) It took a negative view of social media.
   (b) It focused on social media among young people.
   (c) It concluded that social media spread news quickly.
   (d) It showed how social media companies grew.

4. For what has Joel Medford earned other people's admiration?

   (a) his range of publications
   (b) his computing skills
   (c) his grown-up attitude
   (d) his willingness to teach others

5. What would Joel Medford be able to work on at Carolinas Media?

   (a) a line of student magazines
   (b) an array of online publications
   (c) a selection of university websites
   (d) a number of periodicals for academics

6. In the context of the passage, garnered means _____.

   (a) collated
   (b) won
   (c) bought
   (d) harvested

7. In the context of the passage, titles means _____.

   (a) books
   (b) names
   (c) descriptions
   (d) identities

Jodi Macklin
1515 Union Street
Lafayette, IN 47904

Dear Ms. Macklin:

On behalf of everyone here at Homeland, we would like to thank you for being a loyal customer.
As you may have heard, Homeland has had to make the difficult choice to close down a number
of retail stores around the country.

Unfortunately, it has become necessary to take this action, which we believe will improve the
company's financial health in the long term. It saddens us to have to conclude our business in
these communities. However, we must focus our efforts on building a stronger business for
the future. The retail industry as a whole is facing a period of recession and we hope that these
closures will allow us to overcome these challenges.

To make sure we leave on good terms, we plan to conduct several clearance sales. Sale events
will begin on October 1 and continue until the end of the year. Most of the products, including
gardening products and bathroom items, will be 75% off, while tools and DIY equipment will
be offered at half price. Note that there will be a buy-one-get-one-free offer on selected lighting
fixtures.

Select stores will of course remain open in the <u>succeeding</u> months, as will our website. In
addition, we will continue to honor special privileges afforded to members of our loyalty
program. For instance, members will have the chance to purchase sale items one day before each
sale event opens to the public.

We will be <u>disclosing</u> more details about the sale and the closures on our website,
www.homelandstore.com. For additional information, you may call our customer hotline at
1-800-555-4663.

Sincerely,

Harold Corbett
Membership Manager
Homeland

8. What did Homeland announce?

(a) that it is expanding its network of stores
(b) that it is holding an event to thank customers
(c) that it introduced a new membership program
(d) that it decided to shut down some locations

9. What is Homeland hoping to do by its recent action?

(a) attract new investment
(b) enhance its financial fitness
(c) repay outstanding debt
(d) increase the price of its stock

10. What could Homeland's experience be saying about the retail industry in general?

(a) It is a highly profitable industry.
(b) It is mainly becoming an online business.
(c) It is experiencing a financial downturn.
(d) It is suffering from a lack of locations.

11. Which items will be discounted by 50%?

(a) gardening products
(b) bathroom items
(c) tools and DIY equipment
(d) lighting and homeware

12. According to the letter, which is true about members of Homeland's loyalty program?

(a) They can shop before other customers.
(b) They will be given free bed and bath products.
(c) They have exclusive access to some items.
(d) They can buy things at a members-only website.

13. In the context of the passage, succeeding means _____.

(a) winning
(b) previous
(c) following
(d) immediate

14. In the context of the passage, disclosing means _____.

(a) hiding
(b) concluding
(c) telling
(d) disguising

April 14, 2022

Customer Service Department
Major Telecoms
Toronto, Canada

To Whom It May Concern,

I want to express my gratitude for the helpfulness shown by one of your staff members when I visited your main office in Edmonton last week.

I'd gone there to settle an outstanding bill and to request that my line be reconnected. Even though neglecting to pay the bill was a lapse on my part—I simply forgot to do it because I've been busy with my job—I was not happy about losing my connection and having to travel to your office on a weekday.

Nevertheless, the person who attended to me, Michelle Talbot, was extremely kind and considerate. She explained why I needed to be there in person and, after making sure I was the owner of the account in question, processed my overdue payment and reconnected my line in minutes.

In addition to dealing with my problem, Ms. Talbot explained how, should I ever have issues again in the future, I could try resolving them at a branch office or retail store closer to me. She then helped me set up automatic payments on your website to ensure I never miss another. I have tried doing this before on your website but always given up in frustration. This is one area you might improve on.

Overall, Ms. Talbot was not only polite and professional, but, most notably, went above and beyond in anticipating my needs. I hope you will recognize her for this and consider my humble suggestion as well. Thank you.

Sincerely,
Estelle Viera

15. What is the main purpose of Estelle Viera's letter to Major Telecoms?

(a) to inquire about a phone line
(b) to acknowledge an employee at an office
(c) to confirm the terms of a contract
(d) to clarify the steps in a procedure

16. Why did Ms. Viera neglect to pay her bill?

(a) She did not receive a statement.
(b) She sent payment to the wrong address.
(c) She did not have funds to cover the cost.
(d) She was occupied with work.

17. What is the most likely reason that Ms. Viera had to visit Major Telecoms' main office?

(a) It was the closest office to her home.
(b) She had to settle a payment in cash.
(c) Her identity needed to be verified.
(d) She had to pick up a replacement phone.

18. According to Ms. Viera, how can Major Telecoms improve?

(a) by opening additional locations
(b) by extending credit to customers
(c) by making its website easier to use
(d) by offering automatic payments as an option

19. What about Ms. Talbot impressed Ms. Viera the most?

(a) her capacity for foresight
(b) her personable nature
(c) her professional efficiency
(d) her technical knowledge

20. In the context of the passage, lapse means _____.

(a) pause
(b) interruption
(c) decline
(d) mistake

21. In the context of the passage, resolving means _____.

(a) balancing
(b) leveling
(c) addressing
(d) comforting

The Grand Hotel Monaco
Place du Casino,
98003 Monaco

To Whom it May Concern:

I have recently booked two rooms in your hotel through the discount offer on your website, and would like to make some additional requests regarding my stay, which was not possible to do online.

Firstly, I would like to have rooms on the highest floor if possible. The hotel has a rooftop pool and our proximity to that is important because we want to swim a lot. Also, I am staying with my husband and two teenage children, who need supervision, so we need two rooms that are connected by an interior door. We have reserved two double rooms with ocean views, but are willing to have two king-sized rooms, or rooms with city views if that makes it easier. We can also try two queen-sized rooms if necessary.

We also need to request a pick-up service from the airport, which your website says you provide. We will be traveling to Monaco from Nice-Côte d'Azur Airport. Our flight from Madrid lands at 3:45 P.M. on the 3rd of June. Would a hotel bus or car be able to meet us at the airport? It would need space for four people and four or five large suitcases so the car shouldn't be too small.

Finally, we have booked the buffet breakfast for the duration of our stay, but I need to confirm that our dietary requirements will be met. My eldest child and I are vegetarian, so we cannot eat any meat-based products at all. Can you confirm that you will serve vegetarian options? Dairy and gluten are fine for us. Also, could you recommend any restaurants that offer vegetarian options? Many thanks for your help.

Yours sincerely,

Yvonne Lowry

22. Why did Yvonne Lowry write to the hotel staff?

    (a) to confirm her booking with the hotel
    (b) to alert them to a problem with the website
    (c) to ask them about the possibility of a discount
    (d) to inform them of some of her requirements

23. Based on the letter, why most likely does Yvonne Lowry want rooms with a connecting door?

    (a) She wants to share a room with her children.
    (b) She wants to utilize the facilities in two rooms.
    (c) She wants rooms with a separate bedroom and living room.
    (d) She wants her children to be accessible.

24. What sort of rooms has Lowry booked?

    (a) two king-sized rooms with ocean views
    (b) a city-view double and a queen
    (c) two double rooms with views of the sea
    (d) a pair of king-sized rooms looking over the city

25. How would Lowry prefer to get to the hotel?

    (a) by taking a train from Madrid
    (b) by taking the subway from the airport
    (c) by taking a bus from Monaco
    (d) by taking a large vehicle from Nice

26. What does the Lowry family need in the buffet?

    (a) a meat option with no vegetables in it
    (b) a number of gluten-free products
    (c) a selection of non-meat items
    (d) a range of products for dairy-free diners

27. In the context of the passage, proximity means _____.

    (a) nearness
    (b) immediacy
    (c) convenience
    (d) remoteness

28. In the context of the passage, offer means _____.

    (a) donate
    (b) sell
    (c) assign
    (d) discount

Ms. Meredith Collins
President
Greenie Consulting
42 Sterling Road
Minchinbury, NSW 2770

Dear Ms. Collins:

I represent the Sydney Association of Business Owners (SABO), a collective of over 6,000 dues-paying members. SABO is one of the longest-serving organizations for business owners in New South Wales, having <u>originated</u> over 42 years ago. On the first Thursday of every month, we hold a private breakfast seminar on a different topic of interest to our members. We are organizing a seminar for Thursday, December 4, and would like to invite you to present.

In this session, we want to discuss the ways in which businesses can adapt to changing climate conditions. This is a field you have expertise in, as your TV appearances on Channel 4's Morning Show have shown. Here is the full schedule. As you can see, the session will <u>conclude</u> with a panel discussion, which you are also welcome to take part in. It would allow you to talk to some local business leaders.

Schedule:
- 8:00 A.M. ~ 9:00 A.M. – Breakfast / Networking
- 9:00 A.M. ~ 10:00 A.M. – Presentation
- 10:00 A.M. ~ 10:15 A.M. – Audience Questions
- 10:15 A.M. ~ 10:30 A.M. – Break
- 10:30 A.M. ~ 11:30 A.M. – Panel Discussion (with NSW business leaders)

Our seminars tend to attract large numbers of members and you are welcome to hand out promotional material at the event. Enclosed is a copy of our standard agreement for presenters, which includes your fee. As a business owner yourself, you are also entitled to join SABO as a member. I can provide additional details on your request.

If you have any questions, you may contact me by phone at 555-9123 or by e-mail at l.foster@sabo.org. It would be a tremendous honor to have you as a speaker, and I look forward to hearing from you soon.

Warmest regards,

Linda Foster
Organizing Committee
Sydney Association of Business Owners

29. Why did Linda Foster write Meredith Collins a letter?

(a) to ask her to publicize a forthcoming event
(b) to invite her to sign up for the association
(c) to request that she speak at a gathering
(d) to see if she can help with organizing a seminar

30. Based on the letter, which is true about Meredith Collins?

(a) She is well-known internationally.
(b) She planned to visit Sydney in December.
(c) She teaches a course on environmentalism.
(d) She has been a guest on a television program.

31. What is NOT included in the schedule for the breakfast seminar?

(a) a time for meeting other guests
(b) a question and answer session
(c) a presentation from a SABO leader
(d) a discussion with company heads

32. Why most likely does Linda Foster mention the number of participants at a coming event?

(a) to indicate how many seats are available to reserve
(b) to show how Meredith Collins might benefit from participating
(c) to provide an idea of the costs involved in holding it
(d) to suggest that a location is large enough to accommodate a group

33. What can Linda Foster provide on Meredith Collins's request?

(a) help with renting a vehicle
(b) information about membership
(c) reimbursement of her fee
(d) schedules of upcoming meetings

34. In the context of the passage, originated means _____.

(a) started
(b) introduced
(c) revealed
(d) planned

35. In the context of the passage, conclude means _____.

(a) end
(b) include
(c) summarize
(d) commence

정답·해석·해설 p.53

PART 4에서 선별한 다음의 지텔프 빈출 어휘들을 암기한 후 퀴즈로 확인해보세요.

propose v. 제안하다	**assistance** n. 도움
partnership n. 제휴	**organization** n. 기관
firm n. 회사, 기업	**merger** n. 합병
facilitate v. 용이하게 하다	**agreement** n. 합의
convey v. 전달하다	**approve** v. 승인하다
investment n. 투자	**claim** n. 청구, 주장
execute v. 수행하다	**rude** adj. 무례한
fund v. 자금을 대다 n. 자금	**blame** n. 탓, 책임
personnel n. 인적 자원, 직원	**adequately** adv. 제대로, 적절히
approach n. 방법, 접근법	**associate** n. 동료
recruit v. 채용하다	**compensation** n. 보상
supervise v. 감독하다	**refund** n. 환불
enclosed adj. 동봉된	**division** n. 부서
condition n. 조건, 상태	**lack** n. 부족
ownership n. 소유권	**cooperation** n. 협력
efficiency n. 효율성	**workload** n. 업무량
invite v. 초대하다	**responsibility** n. 책임

Quiz 각 단어의 알맞은 뜻을 찾아 연결하세요.

01 merger	ⓐ 채용하다	06 associate	ⓗ 보상
	ⓑ 합병		ⓘ 용이하게 하다
02 investment	ⓒ 환불	07 facilitate	ⓙ 협력
03 recruit	ⓓ 승인하다	08 efficiency	ⓚ 동봉된
	ⓔ 투자		ⓛ 책임
04 workload	ⓕ 업무량	09 compensation	ⓜ 효율성
05 refund	ⓖ 탓, 책임	10 responsibility	ⓝ 동료

정답 01 ⓑ 02 ⓔ 03 ⓐ 04 ⓕ 05 ⓒ 06 ⓝ 07 ⓘ 08 ⓜ 09 ⓗ 10 ⓛ

admit v. 허락하다, 받아들이다

competitive adj. 경쟁을 하는

editorial adj. 편집의

qualification n. 자질, 자격

analysis n. 분석

reveal v. 설명하다, 밝혀내다

argument n. 논거

relevant adj. 관련있는, 적절한

genuine adj. 진심 어린, 진실한

inquire v. 묻다, 알아보다

retail adj. 소매의

recession n. 불황기, 후퇴

overcome v. 극복하다

clearance sale phr. 재고 정리 할인 행사

disclose v. 발표하다, 드러내다

debt n. 빚

downturn n. 침체

exclusive adj. 독점적인

gratitude n. 감사

considerate adj. 사려 깊은

resolve v. 해결하다

polite adj. 예의 바른, 공손한

clarify v. 명확하게 하다

verify v. 확인하다, 입증하다

book v. 예약하다

request n. 요청 v. 요청하다

vegetarian n. 채식주의자

alert v. 알리다

expertise n. 전문 지식

standard adj. 표준의, 보통의

fee n. 강연료, 수수료

tremendous adj. 대단한, 엄청난

publicize v. 홍보하다

accommodate v. 수용하다

Quiz 각 단어의 알맞은 뜻을 찾아 연결하세요.

01 accommodate	ⓐ 진심 어린, 진실한		06 publicize	ⓗ 자격	
02 admit	ⓑ 극복하다		07 resolve	ⓘ 불황기, 후퇴	
	ⓒ 수용하다			ⓙ 홍보하다	
03 genuine	ⓓ 독점적인		08 qualification	ⓚ 요청; 요청하다	
	ⓔ 허락하다			ⓛ 논거	
04 book	ⓕ 대단한, 엄청난		09 retail	ⓜ 해결하다	
05 exclusive	ⓖ 예약하다		10 request	ⓝ 소매의	

정답 01 ⓒ 02 ⓔ 03 ⓐ 04 ⓖ 05 ⓓ 06 ⓙ 07 ⓜ 08 ⓗ 09 ⓝ 10 ⓚ

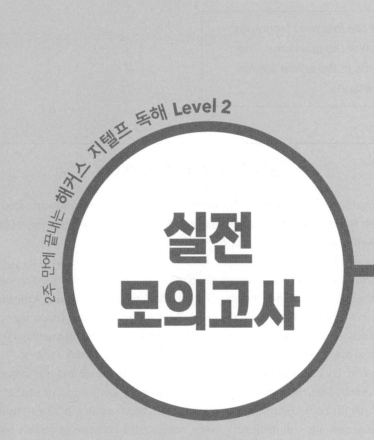

2주 만에 끝내는 해커스 지텔프 독해 Level 2

실전
모의고사

PART 1. Read the following biography article and answer the questions. The underlined words in the article are for vocabulary questions.

LOUIS ARMSTRONG

Louis Armstrong was an American musician and composer whose musical career spanned five decades. He is best recognized for his unmistakable voice, and for being one of the most prominent and influential figures in the history of jazz.

Armstrong was born on August 4, 1901, in New Orleans, Louisiana, to Mary Albert and William Armstrong. After his father left the family, he was taken in by the Karnoffskys, a family of Lithuanian Jews. While traveling with the Karnoffskys, the young Armstrong played a tin horn to attract customers to the family's sales wagon. When Armstrong was 11, he dropped out of school and joined a boys' quartet that sang in the streets for money. At this time, he also learned to play the cornet as an apprentice of jazz trumpeter Bunk Johnson.

However, one day he got in trouble for shooting a gun into the air and was sentenced to a detention center. There he practiced his cornet skills in the camp band, of which he was band master. After his release, Armstrong played in brass band parades in New Orleans. This continued until Armstrong, still in his early teens, attracted the attention of notable people such as Kid Ory, the head of one of the most famous bands in New Orleans. Ory hired Armstrong in 1919, which helped to turn him into a local celebrity.

Armstrong moved to Chicago in 1922, where he landed a job with King Oliver's Creole Jazz Band, earning enough money to quit working in the daytime. He also recorded his first studio recordings for Gennett Records there. Over the next few decades, Armstrong recorded many more records and went on exhaustive tours both domestically and overseas. He produced 19 top-ten hits in his career, two of which reached number one while he was in his 60s, a rare occurrence for a musician that old.

With increasing fame, Armstrong made appearances in film and on television. Most of these were cameos, such as his role as a band leader in the film version of the musical *Hello, Dolly!* Despite his busy schedule, and against his doctor's advice, Armstrong continued to tour and perform live extensively. Following a performance in March, 1971, he suffered a cardiac arrest. While in recovery in July of that same year, he died in his sleep of a second heart attack.

1. What is Louis Armstrong widely known for?

   (a) his unique vocal sound
   (b) being the best trumpeter of his generation
   (c) composing songs for jazz artists
   (d) his musical performances at a young age

2. How did Armstrong earn money in his youth?

   (a) by selling music equipment
   (b) by playing his cornet in the streets
   (c) by joining a singing group for boys
   (d) by giving music lessons

3. What event helped to make Armstrong locally famous?

   (a) being sent to a detention center
   (b) becoming camp band master
   (c) playing music in local parades
   (d) getting hired by Kid Ory

4. According to the passage, what was unusual about some of Armstrong's hit songs?

   (a) They were recorded live during tours.
   (b) They were made by the same recording agency.
   (c) They were popular both domestically and abroad.
   (d) They were produced relatively late in his life.

5. What most likely did Armstrong's doctor tell him?

   (a) to appear less in film and on TV
   (b) to stop going on tour
   (c) to take cardiac medicine
   (d) to get more regular sleep

6. In the context of the passage, apprentice means _____.

   (a) trainee
   (b) helper
   (c) teacher
   (d) master

7. In the context of the passage, landed means _____.

   (a) arrived
   (b) offered
   (c) brought
   (d) got

PART 2. Read the following magazine article and answer the questions. The underlined words in the article are for vocabulary questions.

WEARABLE TECH PROMISES IMPROVED SLEEP

Researchers at the University of Massachusetts Amherst have developed a set of "smart" pajamas fitted with sensors that can monitor a wearer's heart rate, breathing, and posture. Its aim is to provide information that consumers and clinicians alike can use to improve sleep patterns.

Known as the "Phyjama," the garment is one more example of the growing trend toward embedding sensor technology in everyday items. The team behind the Phyjama, led by Trisha L. Andrew, Ph.D., presented its results at the American Chemical Society's Spring 2019 National Meeting & Exposition.

The Phyjama features five sensor-equipped textile patches positioned throughout the garment. These first-of-their-kind patches are linked to each other using silver-plated nylon threads wrapped in cotton. Wires also connect each patch to a printed circuit board built into a Bluetooth transmitter that is the size of a pajama button. The transmitter can send any collected data wirelessly to a receiver, including, potentially, a user's smart watch or phone.

Realizing the project involved some technical challenges. The highly sensitive sensors had to be integrated into the fabric of a garment without adversely affecting the feel, comfort, and function of regular pajamas. In addition, signals from the sensors had to be translated into data users could easily interpret for themselves. Lastly, the pajamas had to be able to withstand multiple wears and washes.

Although the Phyjama was made to be used in scientific sleep research, it has also been targeted for commercial retail. The National Sleep Foundation estimates that profits in the sleep industry are somewhere close to $29 billion. The Phyjama hopes to carve out a place in this industry by advertising its rich data, portability, and the capacity to simultaneously monitor posture, respiration, and heart signals in sleep. Competitors who make similarly smart beds and wristbands combine some but not all of the same benefits in a single product.

Currently, Andrew's team has completed testing and is in the process of securing patents. Once it partners with a manufacturer, it expects to have a product on store shelves within two years, with an estimated retail price between $100 and $200. The researchers are also working on other potential uses of their technology. The team believes wearable sensors that can detect whether a user in motion has lost balance could be applicable in nursing homes and retirement centers.

8. According to the article, what have researchers been working on?

   (a) a study on how gadget use affects people's sleep patterns
   (b) a sensor that monitors brain chemistry during rest periods
   (c) an electronic device that can be worn while asleep
   (d) a report on how sleep quality has changed over time

9. How does the Phyjama communicate the information that it gathers?

   (a) by transmitting it wirelessly
   (b) by printing it out
   (c) by broadcasting audible sounds
   (d) by displaying it on a built-in screen

10. Based on the passage, what was NOT a consideration during the Phyjama's development?

    (a) product durability
    (b) user comfort
    (c) ease of use
    (d) aesthetic design

11. Why do Phyjama's creators probably want to commercialize the product?

    (a) to take advantage of a sizeable market
    (b) to fund further research and development
    (c) to promote awareness of sleep problems
    (d) to attract potential partner manufacturers

12. What does Ms. Andrew's team expect to happen within a two-year period?

    (a) agreements being reached with manufacturers
    (b) customers buying Phyjamas in stores
    (c) orders coming in from nursing homes
    (d) sensors becoming more affordable

13. In the context of the passage, challenges means _____.

    (a) threats
    (b) problems
    (c) objections
    (d) conflicts

14. In the context of the passage, applicable means _____.

    (a) ready
    (b) related
    (c) suitable
    (d) legitimate

MONOPOLY

Monopoly is a real-estate board game in which individuals compete for control of properties, which they use to bankrupt opponents and dominate the game. Published by Hasbro, it is the best-selling privately patented board game in history.

The game is named for the economic concept whereby a single company maintains total control of a market. It is derived from an earlier board game called The Landlord's Game, created in 1903 by Lizzie G. Magie. Magie's game grew popular enough that others devised homemade variations to play with friends. Charles B. Darrow, intrigued by one of these versions, modeled his own and called it Monopoly. From 1933 to 1934, he successfully marketed his game to retailers. Unfortunately, game sales <u>exceeded</u> his production capacity and he sold the rights to Parker Brothers in 1935.

To play the game, players start with a fixed amount of play money issued by a designated banker. They roll a pair of dice to see who goes first and to move game pieces around the board. Along the way, players buy up vacant properties, which they may trade to complete matching sets. Having a completed set creates a monopoly and means improvements like houses or hotels can be added. Players must pay rent on properties <u>occupied</u> by an opponent, and rents go up with every improvement. Players who cannot afford the payments eventually go bankrupt and are removed from the game. The game continues until one player remains. The board also features event squares that instruct players to perform specific tasks.

Despite involving elements of strategy and negotiation, Monopoly has earned criticism for its game mechanics. Many games take too long to finish. In addition, the game's dependence on chance means one or two lucky players accumulate resources early on and become "runaway leaders," players who advance so quickly that others have no way of catching up.

Still, the game has become a mainstay in homes around the world, spawning hundreds of editions. In the original sets, properties were named for streets in Atlantic City, New Jersey. In some countries, these and other features may be altered to suit the local market.

15. What is the object of the game in Monopoly?

   (a) to dominate a property market
   (b) to earn the most money per round
   (c) to endure until all opponents give up
   (d) to build a fixed number of houses

16. Where did Darrow most likely get the idea for Monopoly?

   (a) from being introduced to Lizzie Magie
   (b) from playing an early version with friends
   (c) from creating The Landlord's Game
   (d) from working briefly at Parker Brothers

17. Which is true about the way Monopoly is played?

   (a) Whoever has the most money goes first.
   (b) Designated bankers use a special game piece.
   (c) Only properties in complete sets can be improved.
   (d) Players draw cards to move around the board.

18. What are "runaway leaders"?

   (a) players who develop a big lead early in a game
   (b) players who leave a game despite being ahead
   (c) players who refuse to quit no matter how long it takes
   (d) players who always seem to come in second place

19. How is Monopoly probably different in other countries?

   (a) Players use real money.
   (b) The game board is larger.
   (c) There are fewer game pieces.
   (d) Street names are changed.

20. In the context of the passage, exceeded means _____.

   (a) competed
   (b) outspent
   (c) enlarged
   (d) surpassed

21. In the context of the passage, occupied means _____.

   (a) employed
   (b) controlled
   (c) engaged
   (d) liberated

January 14, 2022

Margot Floyd
42 Michele St
Milwaukee, WI 53224

Dear Ms. Floyd,

I am writing to follow up on your previous request. When we last met, you had inquired about hiring me to train your daughter, Judy, in preparation for her audition to the Winkler College of Performing Arts.

I reviewed Judy's demonstration tape and agree that she has the talent to pursue a career in dance. That said, I <u>noticed</u> some habits that will need to be corrected. I would recommend she begin classes here immediately after graduating high school so as not to hamper what progress she has already made.

Our studio is open six days a week from 8 A.M. to 8 P.M., Monday to Saturday, and is regularly staffed by six instructors, including myself. Early mornings are reserved for our youngest students, while career dancers come from 9 A.M. to 4 P.M. We teach older, school-age children until 6 P.M. and leave the last two hours for working adults and hobbyists. Most class sizes are <u>confined</u> to between 12 and 20 students to ensure a suitable pupil-teacher ratio.

For Judy, classes will probably consist of rehearsals of different poses, moves, and steps that gradually and progressively increase in difficulty. On occasion, she will be asked to perform short routines to demonstrate the new skills she's acquired, with teachers providing specific and personalized feedback. If you like, you may book a private coach to supplement her learning or provide more intensive instruction. I know of other instructors outside the school who might fit the bill. I can provide you with their information anytime you require it.

Please contact me at 555-2393 if you have any concerns or to make an appointment for a more detailed consultation.

Sincerely,
Debbie Lundgren
Lundgren Dance Academy

22. Why did Debbie Lundgren write Margot Floyd a letter?

    (a) to ask about taking some classes
    (b) to respond to an earlier inquiry
    (c) to report on a student's progress
    (d) to confirm details of an appointment

23. How can Ms. Lundgren help Judy Floyd?

    (a) by teaching her basic skills
    (b) by designing a special routine
    (c) by replacing bad tendencies
    (d) by helping her choose a college

24. When could Judy probably take a class?

    (a) in the early morning
    (b) in the late afternoon
    (c) in the late morning
    (d) in the early evening

25. What will Judy be expected to do?

    (a) Formulate some dance moves for a class
    (b) Request personalized feedback from instructors
    (c) Give brief exhibitions of what she has learned
    (d) Attend regular rehearsals for a final presentation

26. Why most likely does Ms. Lundgren mention outside instructors?

    (a) She is considering hiring additional instructors.
    (b) She wants to illustrate how those at her school are better.
    (c) She is concerned that a class has no room for additional students.
    (d) She believes they could complement what Judy will learn at the school.

27. In the context of the passage, noticed means _____.

    (a) detected
    (b) adjusted
    (c) revealed
    (d) described

28. In the context of the passage, confined means _____.

    (a) cramped
    (b) limited
    (c) invested
    (d) enclosed

정답·해석·해설 p.63

PART 1. Read the following biography article and answer the questions. The underlined words in the article are for vocabulary questions.

RALPH LAUREN

Ralph Lauren is an American businessman and fashion designer famous for his tremendous contributions to the global fashion industry. He is the executive chairman and chief creative officer of the Ralph Lauren Corporation.

Lauren was born Ralph Lifshitz on October 14, 1939, in the Bronx, New York, to Jewish immigrants Frieda and Frank Lifshitz. He grew up in a modest working-class apartment where he shared a cramped bedroom with two older siblings. Growing up, Lauren became known as a well-dressed young man among his peers, who mostly preferred T-shirts and jeans. His appreciation for pricey clothes led him to take part-time jobs so he could spend his <u>wages</u> on name-brand attire.

At 16, Lauren changed his surname because other youths made fun of his foreign-sounding birth name. He graduated from high school and later enrolled at the City University of New York, where he majored in business. However, he did not satisfy the requirements for a degree and dropped out after two years. Then he served time in the United States Army from 1962 to 1964.

Following his military duty, Lauren got a job at Brooks Brothers, the oldest men's clothier in the United States. Brooks Brothers was a logical choice because it focused on the preppy, Ivy League look that Lauren had always admired. However, failing to convince Brooks Brothers to consider his own forward-looking designs, Lauren decided to go out on his own.

Lauren pitched his ideas to several companies but did not succeed. Eventually, he persuaded Beau Brummel, a manufacturer of neckties, to back him. In 1967, Ralph Lauren launched his own line of ties. The following year, he expanded into other types of menswear and named his collection "Polo," reflecting his interest in sports. By 1969, Lauren attained his first significant breakthrough when he obtained an exclusive contract to sell his menswear line at luxury department store Bloomingdale's. Lauren continued to build on this success, winning a Coty American Fashion Critics' Award in 1970 and opening his first stand-alone Polo store in Beverly Hills in 1971.

Polo has since become a multi-billion-dollar international corporation and has branched out into women's clothes, handbags, and fragrances. Today, having realized his lifelong <u>aspiration</u> to become an established fashion designer, Lauren has expanded his interests. He is an avid collector of luxury automobiles and is also heavily involved in charity work.

1. What is Ralph Lauren best known for?

   (a) his interest in fashion as a youth
   (b) creating unprecedented fashion designs
   (c) his impact on the world of fashion
   (d) developing new methods of fashion manufacture

2. Why did Lauren work in part-time jobs as a child?

   (a) He had younger siblings to support.
   (b) He wanted to imitate his popular friends.
   (c) He hoped to save up for an apartment.
   (d) He needed money to buy expensive clothes.

3. When did Lauren leave Brooks Brothers?

   (a) when he returned to college to finish his degree
   (b) when he did not satisfy conditions of his contract
   (c) when he received a better business offer
   (d) when they would not consider his designs

4. What most likely led to Lauren's partnership with Beau Brummel?

   (a) being turned down by other companies repeatedly
   (b) the large production capacity of the manufacturer
   (c) failing to sell his own line of neckties
   (d) the marketing potential of a well-known brand

5. What was the first big turning point in Lauren's career?

   (a) coming up with a catchy brand name
   (b) getting a contract with Bloomingdale's
   (c) being named the Coty Award winner
   (d) opening a Polo shop in Beverly Hills

6. In the context of the passage, wages means _____.

   (a) salary
   (b) debts
   (c) credit
   (d) resources

7. In the context of the passage, aspiration means _____.

   (a) attention
   (b) reputation
   (c) ambition
   (d) imagination

PART 2. Read the following magazine article and answer the questions. The underlined words in the article are for vocabulary questions.

SOCIAL STYLES MODEL

Research developed in the 1960s by psychologists David Merrill and Roger Reid suggests that there are four distinct personality types or social styles that describe how people interact in business settings. These types are illustrated by the Social Styles Model.

According to the Social Styles Model, most people will display one of four social styles—analytical, driving, amiable, and expressive—depending on a combination of their assertiveness and responsiveness. Assertive individuals are more likely to tell and direct rather than to ask or listen, while responsive people are more likely to be people-oriented rather than task-oriented. Associated with each personality type is a range of behavioral traits that give some insight into how each one might think, communicate, and collaborate.

For instance, analytical people are both unassertive and unresponsive. Often perceived as cold, they tend to be reasonable, orderly, and methodical, and prefer to evaluate facts or data before acting. They thrive in structured environments, but may respond poorly to stress or rapid changes.

People with a driving style are assertive but unresponsive. They like to get things done quickly and for this reason make efficient leaders. They will <u>persist</u> with a task even if others don't agree with it. Colleagues and subordinates may find it challenging to cope with their unemotional style and lack of concern for others.

Amiable personalities are unassertive but responsive. They strive to maintain good relations and avoid conflict whenever possible. Although <u>reliable</u> as individuals and supportive of others, they can be resistant to change and lack initiative.

Lastly, expressive people tend to be both assertive and responsive. Outgoing and enthusiastic, they thrive on stimulation and despise routine. They can be inspiring and motivational leaders at their best, but impulsive and manipulative at their worst.

In applying the Social Styles Model at work, it is important to remember that not everyone may fit neatly into one category. Most people will show dominant traits in one of the four, but they may also adopt different styles based on who they are interacting with. This is why knowledge of the Social Styles Model can be useful in such matters as business negotiations, hiring, and team formation, where it can help to create more satisfactory outcomes and a harmonious workplace environment.

8. What is the article mainly about?

   (a) policies that improve staff productivity
   (b) practices that help to motivate employees
   (c) techniques for communicating with personnel
   (d) behaviors displayed by people in the workplace

9. Based on the article, what determines people's social styles?

   (a) their cultural and family background
   (b) their education and social upbringing
   (c) their assertiveness and responsiveness
   (d) their personal beliefs and motivations

10. Why are people with driving personalities difficult to work with?

    (a) They lack specific leadership skills.
    (b) They ignore other people's feelings.
    (c) They burn out quickly from working too hard.
    (d) They like to argue with others about their ideas.

11. Which of the following conditions would most likely be unsuitable for expressive personalities?

    (a) having fixed work hours
    (b) leading large teams
    (c) dealing with frequent changes
    (d) speaking in public

12. What could be a benefit for companies that use the Social Styles Model?

    (a) greater company loyalty
    (b) enhanced public image
    (c) better staff cooperation
    (d) faster product development

13. In the context of the passage, persist means _____.

    (a) protect
    (b) continue
    (c) dismantle
    (d) amend

14. In the context of the passage, reliable means _____.

    (a) truthful
    (b) hesitant
    (c) insecure
    (d) dependable

ENIAC

ENIAC, or the Electronic Numerical Integrator and Computer, was the first programmable electronic digital computer that could be modified to meet specific objectives. It was built toward the end of World War II by scientists working under military contract at the University of Pennsylvania's Moore School of Electrical Engineering. It took three years and $400,000 to finish.

Originally, ENIAC was designed to help the US during World War II by calculating values for artillery range tables, or the angles of elevation at which gun barrels must be set in order to strike distant targets. Instructions were relayed not by running programs off a tape, but by a handful of operators manually connecting cables between sockets on a control panel. Once thus "programmed," the machine could complete calculations at electronic speed, giving it an advantage over mechanical devices.

Like similarly advanced computers of its day, ENIAC had conditional branching, a feature which allows a computer to return appropriate results by comparing inputted data sets. A simplified example would be the instruction, IF X = 40 THEN GO TO LINE 18. However, ENIAC could process calculations much faster than any predecessor. It could add or subtract 5,000 times a second, as well as multiply, divide, and find square roots.

ENIAC itself was enormous. It filled an entire basement at the Moore School. It had 40 individual panels, each approximately 0.5 meters wide by 0.5 meters deep by 2.5 meters high, and featured an array of thousands of resistors, capacitors, and other components. Weighing over 25,000 kilograms, it required 200 kilowatts of electrical power, and, thanks to 18,000 vacuum tubes, generated 150 kilowatts of heat when running at capacity.

Unfortunately, by the time of ENIAC's completion in 1946, it was long overdue. World War II had, by then, ended. So, ENIAC was subsequently made to perform calculations for the construction of hydrogen bombs, among other tasks. It was eventually surpassed by smaller, transistor-enabled computers that could store programs and data in memory. Pieces of ENIAC are now on public display at various US institutions, including the University of Pennsylvania and the Smithsonian in Washington, D.C.

15. What was ENIAC?

(a) a military weapon
(b) a university program
(c) an early computer
(d) a government contract

16. Why was ENIAC originally developed?

(a) to perform scientific experiments
(b) to serve the military during battle
(c) to speed up a manufacturing process
(d) to enable cheaper telecommunications

17. What gave ENIAC an advantage over its predecessors?

(a) its smaller size
(b) its memory storage
(c) its operating costs
(d) its processing speed

18. Which was not a characteristic of ENIAC?

(a) It was half a meter wide.
(b) It was extremely heavy.
(c) It consumed a lot of electricity.
(d) It produced heat while in operation.

19. What could be the reason ENIAC was later replaced?

(a) Pieces of it were permanently damaged.
(b) Computers could be built smaller than before.
(c) Supply prices dropped for certain metals.
(d) Public fears grew over nuclear technology.

20. In the context of the passage, relayed means _____.

(a) conveyed
(b) retained
(c) mailed
(d) replaced

21. In the context of the passage, overdue means _____.

(a) payable
(b) delayed
(c) blocked
(d) excessive

PART 4. Read the following business letter and answer the questions. The underlined words in the letter are for vocabulary questions.

Mr. Robert Fuller
6818 Kipling Drive
Holland, OH 43528

Dear Mr. Fuller,

Thank you for stopping by last week to interview for the position of junior architect. I'd like to congratulate you for passing the application process. We would like to offer you the job.

Given your prior experience and qualifications, we strongly feel that you <u>merit</u> a position with the firm. As a junior architect, you will be working on blueprints for various residential building projects. Depending on your progress, you may be assigned to work on other projects such as museums, hotels, shopping centers, and office towers.

During your first year, you will work under the direction of Tom Sloe, one of our senior architects. However, you will also have the opportunity to work with architects Archibald Caldwell and Louisa Lim, the senior partners whom you met during your interview.

As for the starting date, we would prefer that you begin in the first week of April. You will need to take part in a mandatory training process before starting work on any actual projects. This process can take up to two weeks to complete, so that should give you enough time to be ready to take on a project in May.

To confirm your acceptance of this offer, including your agreement to the enclosed terms of employment, please call 555-0294 during regular work hours. Someone from my office will attempt to <u>reach</u> you if we have not received a response by the end of the week. Congratulations once again and we look forward to working with you.

Warmly,

Vera Moss
Vera Moss
Human Resources Manager
Caldwell and Associates

22. Why did Vera Moss write Robert Fuller a letter?

(a) to thank him for attending an event
(b) to praise him for a job well done
(c) to congratulate him on a promotion
(d) to ask him to join as an employee

23. What will Robert Fuller be working on first?

(a) office towers
(b) museum buildings
(c) residential houses
(d) commercial centers

24. Who will be supervising Robert Fuller at work?

(a) Vera Moss
(b) Tom Sloe
(c) Louisa Lim
(d) Archibald Caldwell

25. Why most likely does Ms. Moss prefer to schedule a start date in early April?

(a) Employees must undergo training before actual work begins.
(b) A department is in urgent need of personnel.
(c) A company outing has been planned for the month after.
(d) Conditions require that a project be completed before May.

26. What will happen if Robert Fuller fails to respond to the letter?

(a) His offer will be adjusted.
(b) A start date will be moved.
(c) A representative will phone him.
(d) His position will be given to another candidate.

27. In the context of the passage, merit means _____.

(a) deny
(b) award
(c) benefit
(d) deserve

28. In the context of the passage, reach means _____.

(a) contact
(b) extend
(c) identify
(d) conclude

정답·해석·해설 p.71

PART 1. Read the following biography article and answer the questions. The underlined words in the article are for vocabulary questions.

DAVID FINCHER

David Fincher is an American producer and director working in film, television, and music. With numerous nominations and awards over the span of three decades, Fincher has achieved fame for his continuous pursuit of perfection and remains one of the most sought-after figures in Hollywood.

David Fincher was born on August 28, 1962, in Denver, Colorado, to author Howard Fincher and mental-health nurse Claire Mae. When Fincher was two years old, his family moved to a small town outside San Francisco, where he first developed an interest in film after catching a screening of the immensely successful American western, *Butch Cassidy and the Sundance Kid*. Fincher began making home movies with an 8 mm film camera shortly thereafter.

As a teenager, Fincher resided in Ashland, Oregon, where he participated in numerous extracurricular activities associated with filmmaking, such as directing school plays, working as a projectionist at a movie theater, and taking a job as a production assistant at a local television news station.

Fincher began to realize his dream of a professional film career in the early 1980s, when he was hired as an assistant cameraman for visual effects company Industrial Light & Magic, then owned by George Lucas, the creator of *Star Wars*. He worked on the hit movie *Indiana Jones and the Temple of Doom*, and was commissioned to direct a television ad for the American Cancer Society. In the ad, he shocked viewers by depicting a human fetus smoking a cigarette in its mother's womb. This boldness attracted attention from Hollywood producers, and the recognition prompted Fincher to co-found Propaganda Films in 1986, a video-production company that produced many successful films and music videos between 1990 and 2002.

Fincher's success only grew from there, and he has since won substantial praise and recognition from his industry peers. His work has earned him both nominations and trophies in the Academy Awards, the UK film industry's BAFTAs, and the Golden Globes. A crowning achievement has been winning a Golden Globe for his direction of *The Social Network*, a film about the development of Facebook.

Fincher continues to be active in American cinema. His wife is fellow film producer Ceán Chaffin, who has helped him complete over half a dozen film projects.

1. What is David Fincher most famous for?

   (a) receiving many nominations and awards
   (b) his early interest in directing films
   (c) being highly desired in Hollywood
   (d) his constant quest for perfection

2. What inspired Fincher to become a filmmaker?

   (a) watching a hit movie
   (b) working with his parents
   (c) growing up in San Francisco
   (d) receiving a camera as a gift

3. Which is not true about Fincher in his youth?

   (a) He directed plays for his school.
   (b) He was employed at a movie theater.
   (c) He filmed his first commercial movie.
   (d) He assisted at a TV news station.

4. What made producers in Hollywood notice Fincher?

   (a) his work at Industrial Light & Magic
   (b) making a controversial TV commercial
   (c) his role in the *Indiana Jones* movie
   (d) opening his own successful film company

5. According to the article, what is considered Fincher's highest professional achievement?

   (a) winning a Golden Globe for best director
   (b) directing the 21st century's top music video
   (c) producing the most Oscar-nominated actors
   (d) making one of the first movies about Facebook

6. In the context of the passage, resided means _____.

   (a) relocated
   (b) lived
   (c) consisted
   (d) practiced

7. In the context of the passage, realize means _____.

   (a) create
   (b) notice
   (c) fulfill
   (d) understand

HOW WATCHING FILMS INFLUENCES THE MOODS AND ATTITUDES OF YOUNG PEOPLE

Recent research indicates that the moods and attitudes of young people can be affected by watching movies. According to researchers, this influence may have an impact on how they view certain groups of people in the community.

In laboratory studies, psychologists have implemented a variety of mood induction procedures (MIPs) to create positive, negative, or neutral feelings. Films are particularly successful as MIPs because they can have dynamic characters and plots that are similar to real life, and they can generate intense emotional reactions, such as fear or excitement, that are duplicated in the viewer. Thus, a practical use of film may be to encourage young people to change their attitudes toward certain groups of people, especially those for whom they hold negative views.

One such group is the elderly. Surveys indicate that the majority of young adults have a negative view of old people. They perceive them as being lonely, impatient, dependent, and physically frail. These attitudes are consistent with how older people are often portrayed in movies. What this suggests is that movies may be partially responsible for giving a false impression of the elderly. If so, it might equally be possible for movies that depict the elderly differently to produce an alternative outcome.

To find out how students' attitudes toward old people would change after watching a film, researchers at the Institute of Psychology in Moscow had 70 undergraduate and graduate students watch a film. The average age of the first group was 19, while that of the latter was 24. The film, *The Best Exotic Marigold Hotel*, features elderly actors as entertaining characters in humorous situations.

The results of the assessment fell slightly short of researchers' expectations, however, as the combined groups showed no major change in their views of the elderly. Consequently, the psychologists decided to compare the results of each group. It turned out that among undergraduates, perceptions of the elderly remained largely unchanged. By contrast, the postgraduates evaluated old people more favorably. On 9 out of 25 scales, their ratings changed from negative to positive.

These findings showcase that movies can alter attitudes, although insufficiently in younger groups. Further research could consider what other factors might influence youthful attitudes toward the elderly or whether other programs exist that could help to alter their opinions of the aged.

8. What is the topic of the article?

   (a) the attitudes of young people toward popular films
   (b) the way movies affect the viewpoints of the young
   (c) how movies portray the young and the old
   (d) how young people perceive old people

9. What is a feature that makes films effective as MIPs?

   (a) their authentic scenarios and storylines
   (b) their capacity to provide a multisensory experience
   (c) their production of empathy in the viewer
   (d) their portrayal of reality from a neutral perspective

10. According to surveys, what is true about the sentiment of most young people regarding the elderly?

   (a) They think their ability to learn is limited.
   (b) They do not have a very high opinion of them.
   (c) They generally respect them as their elders.
   (d) They feel their knowledge and skills are outdated.

11. Why most likely did researchers choose *The Best Exotic Marigold Hotel*?

   (a) because it was popular in Moscow when it was released
   (b) because it was not well known among the participants
   (c) because it contains controversial material about old people
   (d) because it presents the elderly in a favorable light

12. What did psychologists learn by comparing the results of the two groups?

   (a) Postgraduates showed no major change in their views of old people.
   (b) Younger people barely altered their views of the elderly.
   (c) Each group changed their opinions on 9 of 25 scales.
   (d) Both of the groups gave positive reviews of the movie.

13. In the context of the passage, duplicated means _____.

   (a) forgotten
   (b) inspired
   (c) repeated
   (d) distracted

14. In the context of the passage, evaluated means _____.

   (a) surveyed
   (b) renewed
   (c) mended
   (d) rated

THE COOPER'S HILL CHEESE-ROLLING AND WAKE

The Cooper's Hill Cheese-Rolling and Wake is a world-famous event in which groups of competitors chase cheese down an extremely steep hill. It is best known for being very dangerous, with competitors often needing medical attention.

There are two competing theories for why the race originally began, neither of which has been proven. Some people claim that holding it was a way of maintaining grazing rights for animals on Cooper's Hill, while others believe that it was connected to the pre-Christian pagan ritual of rolling bundles of burning brushwood down the hill. The first historical evidence of the race being held comes from an 1826 message received by the Gloucester town crier, but the tradition was known to already be very old by that point.

The race features a seven to nine pound circle of Double Gloucester cheese, which, since 1988, has been supplied by cheese maker Diana Smart. The cheese must be encased in wood and decorated with ribbons before a master of ceremony rolls it down the 200-yard, 1:2-gradient hill to start the race. Once the cheese is released the racers run after it and either try to catch it, or be the first to follow it to the bottom of the hill. The cheese can reach speeds of 70 miles per hour, making it potentially dangerous for spectators, so a lightweight foam stand-in has been used instead in some years. Winners of the race are <u>awarded</u> real cheese.

The steepness of the hill, and the speed at which the cheese rolls down it, make injuries a common occurrence in the race. The highest number of injuries was sustained in 1993, when fifteen people were hurt, four seriously. Recently, teams of volunteers have been stationed at the foot of the hill to keep participants safe.

After 15,000 spectators came to the event in 2009, it was canceled by the authorities in 2010. However, local people soon restarted the tradition and now organize the event without any official assistance. Even though police have tried to <u>deter</u> people from taking part, it remains a hugely popular event with both locals and tourists, who come from around the world to experience this quirky English tradition.

15. What is the Cooper's Hill Cheese-Rolling and Wake best known for?

    (a) It is the only cheese-rolling event in England.
    (b) It is held on the steepest hill in the UK.
    (c) It is extremely hazardous to participants.
    (d) It is one of the oldest pagan ceremonies.

16. Why most likely does no one know why the cheese-rolling event started?

    (a) The race was not recorded by the Gloucester town crier.
    (b) The race was started by Christians from other regions.
    (c) The race began a long time ago.
    (d) The race was considered to be against the law.

17. What should be done before the race can begin?

    (a) the consecration of the cheese by a priest
    (b) the adornment of the cheese with ribbons
    (c) the town crier's announcement of the start
    (d) the cheese handed over to the participants

18. Why was the cheese replaced by a foam stand-in?

    (a) because the race was considered too fast
    (b) because the organizers wanted to maintain the cheese
    (c) because racers could not catch the cheese
    (d) because the cheese could have harmed spectators

19. What was probably the reason local people started to organize the race?

    (a) The hill's owner stopped people from racing.
    (b) The safety issues meant few people came.
    (c) The race lost its financial backing.
    (d) The event was officially canceled.

20. In the context of the passage, awarded means _____.

    (a) given
    (b) donated
    (c) allowed
    (d) paid

21. In the context of the passage, deter means _____.

    (a) motivate
    (b) notify
    (c) discourage
    (d) catch

ATTENTION

TO: Loyal Customers of Atlantic Sun Productions
FROM: Diane Harrow of Atlantic Sun Productions - Client Account Services
SUBJECT: Service Offering

Happy New Year! As a longtime client, you are among the first to know about Atlantic Sun Productions' newest service offering. For nearly 20 years, small businesses like yours have relied on Atlantic Sun Productions to create high-quality recorded content for televised advertisements, product videos, training videos, and corporate events. Today, we are pleased to tell you that we are launching an Internet video service beginning in February.

As a growing number of people get their news and entertainment <u>exclusively</u> from the Internet, it becomes crucial that companies learn how to communicate with them on digital media, which presents both advantages and disadvantages. The biggest benefits are reach and cost. Your videos can be seen by more people online than on television, and distributing videos on the Internet is far cheaper than negotiating airtime with broadcasters. However, producing video for the Internet also presents technical challenges involving file formats, sizes, and other restrictions.

Our promise to you is to help you navigate the world of online video by offering production, editing, and distribution services specifically designed for the Internet. Whether you want to add an introductory video to your homepage, send advertisements through email, stream content on other websites, or disseminate training videos to employees in different locations, we have you covered. Plus, we will do all this in a way that <u>remains</u> entirely affordable to you.

Also, you will receive a special one-time discount of $500 on your first Internet video package if you put the order in this month. Call 555-0189 today or email info@atlanticsunprods.com. We hope to hear from you soon!

Sincerely,

Diane Harrow
Client Account Services
Atlantic Sun Productions

22. What is the letter about?

    (a) a deadline for clients to sign up for a deal
    (b) a new company that is offering online video
    (c) the launch of an additional service
    (d) the company's recent online advertisement

23. Which of the following has Atlantic Sun Productions NOT done in the past?

    (a) produced training videos
    (b) worked on movie productions
    (c) created advertisements for television
    (d) documented corporate events on video

24. According to Ms. Harrow, what is a benefit of digital media over traditional media?

    (a) Videos do not have to be produced at high quality.
    (b) Websites allow businesses to create their own videos online.
    (c) Online videos will be seen by a larger audience.
    (d) Negotiating deals with online companies is easier.

25. What advantage does Atlantic Sun Productions most likely offer to companies?

    (a) low production costs
    (b) fast completion times
    (c) networks of actors
    (d) national distribution channels

26. What could be the reason some customers are eligible for a discount?

    (a) signing up on a website
    (b) placing an order within a month
    (c) selecting a special package
    (d) doing some work for Atlantic Sun

27. In the context of the passage, exclusively means _____.

    (a) solely
    (b) partially
    (c) uniquely
    (d) independently

28. In the context of the passage, remains means _____.

    (a) lives
    (b) waits
    (c) departs
    (d) stays

정답·해석·해설 p.79

G-TELP
기출 유의어 리스트

지텔프 독해 영역에서 어휘 문제로 출제된 어휘들과 그 유의어들을 암기할 수 있도록 한 데 모았다.
예문과 함께 각 어휘의 쓰임을 정확히 암기하여 어휘 문제는 100% 잡고 가자!

1
address

대처하다 = manage

Many regions need assistance with **addressing(= managing)** recurring water shortages.
많은 지역들은 반복되는 물 부족 문제에 대처하는 데 도움이 필요하다.

2
administer

실시하다 = perform

The tests were **administered(= performed)** by faculty at the college.
시험은 대학의 교수진에 의해 실시되었다.

3
adopt

받아들이다 = accept

Our firm is prepared to **adopt(= accept)** most of your recommendations.
저희 회사는 당신의 충고 대부분을 받아들일 준비가 되었습니다.

4
advise

권고하다 = recommend

Taking sleeping pills when you are ill is not **advised(= recommended)** by doctors.
아플 때 수면제를 복용하는 것은 의사들에 의해 권고되지 않는다.

5
appear

~인 것 같다 = seem

From a young age, he **appeared(= seemed)** destined to become a star.
어릴 때부터, 그는 스타가 될 운명인 것 같았다.

나타나다 = emerge

As they were looking out to sea, a boat suddenly **appeared(= emerged)** on the horizon.
그들이 바다를 바라보고 있었을 때, 한 척의 배가 갑자기 수평선에 나타났다.

6
assert

주장하다 = claim

Scientists **assert(= claim)** that the experiment results are invalid.
과학자들은 그 실험 결과는 근거가 없다고 주장한다.

7
attain

차지하다 = assume

Anna Wintour **attained(= assumed)** the role of *Vogue*'s editor-in-chief in 1988.
안나 윈투어는 1988년에 「보그」의 편집장 역할을 차지했다.

얻다 = earn

He **attained(= earned)** success in the industry mostly through sheer determination.
그는 거의 순전히 투지로 업계에서 성과를 얻었다.

8
authorize

허가하다 = allow

The university **authorized(= allowed)** the study on the condition that it be conducted on campus.
대학은 연구가 학내에서 시행된다는 조건하에 연구를 허가했다.

9 **back**	**지지하다** = support Davis often used his celebrity to **back(= support)** the civil rights movement. 데이비스는 시민권 운동을 지지하기 위해 종종 자신의 명성을 이용했다.
10 **balloon**	**증가하다** = grow Our sales **ballooned(= grew)** after advertising in your publication. 저희 매출은 당신의 출판물에 광고를 한 후 증가했습니다.
11 **buffer**	**완화하다** = lessen Improving the soil's ability to absorb water will **buffer(= lessen)** the flooding that occurs during heavy rains. 토양의 물 흡수 능력을 개선시키는 것은 폭우 시 발생하는 홍수를 완화할 것이다.
12 **chase**	**쫓다** = drive The sheepdog **chased(= drove)** away a bull that was threatening the sheep. 양치기 개는 양을 위협하던 황소를 쫓아냈다. **따라가다** = follow The police **chased(= followed)** the burglar to the edge of town but couldn't catch him. 경찰은 마을의 끝자락까지 강도를 따라갔지만 그를 잡을 수 없었다.
13 **complement**	**어울리다** = match The music in the film **complements(= matches)** the gloomy atmosphere perfectly. 그 영화의 음악은 우울한 분위기와 완벽하게 어울린다.
14 **complete**	**작성하다** = prepare The CEO **completed(= prepared)** the marketing strategy prior to the meeting with his agency. 최고 경영자는 대행사와의 회의 전에 마케팅 전략을 작성했다. **마치다** = end The pianist **completed(= ended)** his performance and stood up to wave to the crowd. 피아니스트는 연주를 마치고 관중에게 손을 흔들기 위해 일어섰다.
15 **conceal**	**숨기다** = hide The octopus can change its color to **conceal(= hide)** itself from predators. 문어는 포식자에게서 자신을 숨기기 위해 자신의 색을 바꿀 수 있다.
16 **conclude**	**끝나다** = end The study is expected to **conclude(= end)** in five years' time. 연구는 5년 후에 끝날 것으로 예상된다.
17 **contract**	**고용하다** = hire We would like to **contract(= hire)** you to refurbish our main office. 저희는 본사를 재단장하는 데 귀하를 고용하고 싶습니다.

18 **control**	**제어하다** = decrease
	Controlling(= Decreasing) large animal populations was achieved through deliberate hunting. 많은 동물 개체 수를 제어하는 것은 계획적인 사냥을 통해 이루어졌다.

19 **coordinate**	**맞추다** = match
	The couple was famous for **coordinating(= matching)** outfits whenever they went out together. 그 커플은 데이트할 때마다 복장을 맞추는 것으로 유명했다.

20 **cope with**	**맞서다** = deal with
	Despite **coping with(= dealing with)** illness, he remained active for the rest of his career. 병에 맞서고 있었음에도 불구하고, 그는 남은 경력 동안 여전히 활발하게 활동했다.
	처리하다 = manage
	The clerk was struggling to **cope with(= manage)** the constant customer requests. 직원은 끊임없는 고객 요청을 처리하느라 고생하고 있었다.

21 **cover**	**포함하다** = involve
	Future research will have to **cover(= involve)** questions raised by the study. 차후 조사는 연구에서 제기된 문제들을 포함해야 할 것이다.
	이동하다 = travel
	The fastest land animal, the cheetah, can **cover(= travel)** 50 yards in approximately 5 seconds. 가장 빠른 육지 동물인 치타는 약 5초 안에 50야드를 이동할 수 있다.

22 **damage**	**부상을 입다** = injure
	She **damaged(= injured)** her knee performing a stunt for the movie. 그녀는 영화를 위한 스턴트 연기를 하다가 무릎 부상을 입었다.

23 **decline**	**악화되다** = worsen
	The patient's condition **declined(= worsened)** quickly over a three-month period. 환자의 상태는 3개월의 기간 동안 빠르게 악화되었다.

24 **defy**	**거역하다** = disobey
	Muhammad Ali later **defied(= disobeyed)** the US military draft on religious grounds. 무함마드 알리는 후에 종교적인 이유로 미군 징병에 거역했다.

25 deliver	**배송하다** = bring
	I'd like to confirm that we can **deliver(= bring)** the item to the following address. 저희가 다음의 주소로 물품을 배송할 수 있을지 확인하고 싶습니다.
	전하다 = give
	Lincoln **delivered(= gave)** his celebrated speech at Gettysburg in 1863. 링컨은 1863년에 게티즈버그에서 그의 유명한 연설을 전했다.
26 denote	**의미하다** = mean
	The term "zero" comes from an Arabic word **denoting(= meaning)** "nothing." "zero"라는 단어는 "아무것도 아닌 것"을 의미하는 아라비아 단어에서 유래한다.
27 determine	**확인하다** = identify
	A medical team **determined(= identified)** the source of the virus. 의료팀은 바이러스의 근원을 확인했다.
	알게 되다 = learn
	Scientists hope to **determine(= learn)** what causes the strange phenomenon. 과학자들은 그 이상한 현상을 야기하는 것이 무엇인지 알게 되기를 바란다.
28 disrupt	**불안정하게 하다** = unsettle
	The train schedule has been **disrupted(= unsettled)** by the ongoing strike of subway workers. 기차 시간표는 지하철 노동자들의 계속되는 파업으로 인해 불안정하게 되었다.
29 document	**기록하다** = record
	The artist **documented(= recorded)** events from his life in the book *The Andy Warhol Diaries*. 그 예술가는 자신의 일생을 「앤디 워홀 일기」라는 책에 기록했다.
30 excrete	**분비하다** = release
	Waste products **excreted(= released)** by plants are consumed by organisms found in the soil. 식물에 의해 분비되는 노폐물은 흙에서 발견되는 생물들에 의해 소모된다.
31 expand	**팽창하다** = enlarge
	High blood pressure may cause the left side of the heart to **expand(= enlarge)**. 고혈압은 심장의 좌측이 팽창하는 것을 야기할 수 있다.
32 expel	**쫓아내다** = remove
	As a boy, Stallone was **expelled(= removed)** from school for bad behavior. 소년 시절, 스탤론은 나쁜 행동으로 인해 학교에서 쫓겨났다.
33 flock	**모이다** = gather
	Fans of the band **flocked(= gathered)** to buy tickets for their final concert. 그 밴드의 팬들은 그들의 마지막 콘서트 티켓을 사기 위해 모였다.

34 **forecast**	**예측하다** = guess
	Even economists find it difficult to **forecast(= guess)** when another financial recession will come along.
	경제학자들조차 또 다른 경기 침체가 언제 올지 예측하기 어려워한다.

35 **frustrate**	**좌절시키다** = stop
	The Russian winter **frustrated(= stopped)** the advance of Napoleon's army.
	러시아의 겨울은 나폴레옹 군대의 전진을 좌절시켰다.

36 **guarantee**	**보장하다** = ensure
	The company claims that the product will **guarantee(= ensure)** lower electricity usage in the home.
	회사는 그 제품이 가정에서의 더 낮은 전기 사용량을 보장할 것이라고 주장한다.

37 **inspire**	**고무하다** = encourage
	Carl Sagan **inspired(= encouraged)** many young people to pursue careers in science.
	칼 세이건은 많은 젊은이들이 과학 분야의 경력을 추구하도록 고무했다.

38 **land**	**상륙하다** = arrive
	In around 985 A.D., Viking sailors became the first Europeans to **land(= arrive)** in North America.
	서기 985년경에, 바이킹 선원들은 북아메리카에 상륙한 최초의 유럽인이 되었다.
	획득하다 = get
	We **landed(= got)** our first big client in Hardy's Retail 60 years ago.
	저희는 60년 전에 Hardy 소매점이라는 첫 대형 고객을 획득했습니다.

39 **launch**	**나아가게 하다** = propel
	Her role in the film helped to **launch(= propel)** her career into stardom.
	영화에서 그녀의 역할은 그녀의 경력이 스타의 반열로 나아가게 도왔다.

40 **manifest**	**드러내다** = exhibit
	The disease **manifests(= exhibits)** itself as red bumps on the skin.
	그 병은 피부의 붉은 혹으로 스스로를 드러낸다.

41 **offer**	**제공하다** = give
	Our firm can **offer(= give)** you a discount if you complete the purchase by July 31.
	저희 회사는 귀하가 7월 31일까지 구매를 완료하시면 할인을 제공해드릴 수 있습니다.
	판매하다 = sell
	We **offer(= sell)** a range of athletic clothing and equipment for different sports.
	저희는 각양각색의 운동을 위한 다양한 운동복과 운동 기구를 판매합니다.

42 **originate**	**시작되다** = start Buddhism **originated(= started)** in ancient India and then spread east into other parts of Asia. 불교는 고대 인도에서 시작되어 이후 다른 아시아 지역까지 동부로 확산되었다.
43 **perform**	**하다** = do Teachers are blamed when students don't **perform(= do)** well in class and get bad grades. 학생들이 수업에서 잘하지 못하여 좋지 않은 성적을 받으면 선생님들에게 그 탓이 돌아간다. **연기하다** = act He **performed(= acted)** in both the film and stage versions of the story. 그는 그 이야기의 영화 버전뿐만 아니라 공연 버전에서도 연기했다.
44 **persuade**	**설득하다** = convince The director had to be **persuaded(= convinced)** to hire the inexperienced actor. 감독은 경험이 없는 배우를 고용하도록 설득되어야 했다.
45 **plummet**	**떨어지다** = drop After losing power in both its engines, the airplane **plummeted(= dropped)** towards the sea. 두 엔진에서 동력을 잃은 후, 비행기는 바다 쪽으로 떨어졌다.
46 **prohibit**	**금지하다** = disallow Islamic teachings **prohibit(= disallow)** the creation of images of Muhammad. 이슬람의 가르침은 무함마드의 상을 만드는 것을 금지한다.
47 **promote**	**증진하다** = boost The conference aims to **promote(= boost)** trade among countries in the region. 학회는 지역 내 국가 간 무역을 증진하는 것을 목표로 한다. **승진시키다** = raise In 1940, Patton was **promoted(= raised)** to the rank of Brigadier General. 1940년에, 패튼은 준장의 계급으로 승진되었다.
48 **propel**	**밀어내다** = push Volcanic eruptions occur when a buildup of gases **propels(= pushes)** magma to the earth's surface. 화산 폭발은 축적된 가스가 지표면으로 마그마를 밀어낼 때 발생한다.

49 **reach**	**연락하다** = contact You may **reach(= contact)** me through my mobile phone at 555-3094. 귀하는 555-3094로 제 휴대폰에 연락하실 수 있습니다. **닿다** = touch Giraffes have long necks that permit them to **reach(= touch)** the leaves on tall trees. 기린은 높은 나무의 나뭇잎에 닿을 수 있게 해주는 긴 목을 갖고 있다.
50 **recover**	**되찾다** = regain Under his leadership, the nation **recovered(= regained)** territories that had been lost during the war. 그의 지휘하에, 국가는 전쟁 동안 잃었던 영토를 되찾았다. **나아지다** = improve After a week in hospital, his health had **recovered(= improved)** enough that he could walk unaided. 병원에서 한 주를 보낸 후, 그는 도움 없이 걸을 수 있을 만큼 건강이 나아졌다.
51 **reduce**	**줄이다** = cut Through our efforts, we have been able to **reduce(= cut)** the number of product returns. 우리의 노력으로, 반품의 수를 줄일 수 있었습니다.
52 **refuse**	**거절하다** = decline Brad Pitt **refused(= declined)** a number of roles in films that went on to become successful. 브래드 피트는 성공한 영화들의 많은 역할을 거절했다.
53 **remain**	**남다** = stay The heritage hotel has **remained(= stayed)** largely unchanged for over a hundred years. 대대로 상속된 그 호텔은 100년이 넘는 시간 동안 크게 변하지 않고 남아 있다.
54 **renovate**	**개조하다** = remodel The historic building had to be **renovated(= remodeled)** after being partially destroyed by fire. 그 역사적인 건물은 화재로 인해 부분적으로 파괴된 이후 개조되어야 했다.
55 **replace**	**바꾸다** = change Many music aficionados **replaced(= changed)** their record players with CD players in the 1990s. 많은 음악 마니아들은 1990년대에 그들의 전축을 CD 플레이어로 바꾸었다.
56 **satisfy**	**이행하다** = fulfill The studio fired her because she did not **satisfy(= fulfill)** the conditions of her contract. 그 스튜디오는 그녀가 계약 조건을 이행하지 않아 해고했다.

57 see	검사하다 = examine
	A qualified physician **saw(= examined)** the test subjects to verify that the product is safe. 자격을 갖춘 의사가 그 제품이 안전한지 확인하기 위해 시험 대상 물품을 검사했다.
	주목하다 = notice
	The actress was first **seen(= noticed)** by audiences in a television commercial when she was 18. 그 배우는 18살이었을 때 텔레비전 광고에서 시청자들에게 처음으로 주목받았다.

58 segregate	구분 짓다 = differentiate
	Researchers **segregated(= differentiated)** the groups based on their answers to the questions. 연구원들은 집단들을 질문에 대한 그들의 답변에 기반하여 구분 지었다.

59 sense	느끼다 = feel
	She **sensed(= felt)** that her friend was very upset, even though he wasn't showing it. 그녀는 자신의 친구가 속상하다는 것을 드러내지 않았음에도 불구하고 이를 느꼈다.

60 serve	기능을 하다 = function
	The experiments **serve(= function)** to show how the treatment works on different patients. 실험은 다른 환자들에게 치료가 어떻게 작용하는지 보여주는 기능을 한다.

61 shoulder	감당하다 = bear
	He asked his friends to help him **shoulder(= bear)** the cost of recording his first studio album. 그는 자신의 첫 스튜디오 앨범을 녹음하는 비용을 감당하기 위해 친구들에게 도움을 요청했다.

62 solve	해결하다 = correct
	Researchers designed the new study to **solve(= correct)** problems identified in their older studies. 연구원들은 자신들의 지난 연구에서 확인된 문제들을 해결하기 위해 새로운 연구를 설계했다.

63 spot	찾다 = locate
	After being lost for a century, archeologists **spotted(= located)** the sunken ship on a map of the ocean floor. 한 세기 동안 행방불명이 되고 나서야, 고고학자들은 가라앉은 배를 해저 지도에서 찾았다.

64 stage	상연하다 = present
	Despite her fame, she often **staged(= presented)** free performances to support various causes. 그녀의 명성에도 불구하고, 그녀는 다양한 대의를 지지하기 위해 종종 무료 공연을 상연했다.
	기획하다 = organize
	We can **stage(= organize)** a large public event to announce your firm's new product. 저희는 귀사의 새로운 제품을 발표할 큰 공개 행사를 기획할 수 있습니다.

65 **submerge**	**물에 잠기다** = flood
	The town was **submerged(= flooded)** in the 1920s when the reservoir was built in the area. 그 마을은 1920년대에 그 지역에 급수장이 건설되면서 물에 잠겼다.
	숨다 = hide
	The children **submerged(= hid)** themselves in the bush where no one could see them. 아이들은 아무도 자신들을 보지 못하게 덤불 속으로 숨었다.

66 **surpass**	**능가하다** = outdo
	The British Empire **surpassed(= outdid)** all others before it in terms of size. 대영 제국은 규모 면에서 이전의 다른 모든 제국들을 능가했다.

67 **swell**	**부풀다** = bulge
	The volcano **swelled(= bulged)** with magma days before it exploded. 화산은 폭발하기 며칠 전에 마그마로 부풀었다.

68 **transfer**	**옮기다** = remove
	A truck is needed to **transfer(= remove)** the products from the old warehouse. 오래된 창고로부터 제품들을 옮기기 위해 트럭이 필요하다.

69 **vacuum**	**빨아들이다** = inhale
	The whale **vacuumed(= inhaled)** the small fish into its stomach without chewing them. 고래가 작은 물고기들을 씹지 않고 배속으로 빨아들였다.

2. 명사

70 **advancement**	**발달** = improvement
	Newton's work contributed to the **advancement(= improvement)** of physics. 뉴턴의 업적은 물리학의 발달에 기여했다.

71 **aspiration**	**포부** = ambition
	Receiving the Oscar was the fulfillment of her greatest **aspirations (= ambitions)** at the time. 오스카상을 받은 것은 당시 그녀의 가장 큰 포부를 달성한 것이었다.

72 **assumption**	**가정** = guess
	Scientists used the experiment to test their initial **assumptions(= guesses)**. 과학자들은 자신들의 초기 가정을 확인하기 위해 실험을 이용했다.

73 **break**	**휴식 시간** = pause During a **break(= pause)** in the meeting, the management team all ordered coffee from the cafeteria. 회의 중 휴식 시간 동안, 관리팀 모두 매점에서 커피를 주문했다.
74 **case**	**경우** = situation The treatment works in all **cases(= situations)** with incredible results. 그 치료법은 모든 경우에 놀라운 결과로 효과가 있다.
75 **cause**	**원인** = reason Researchers say their findings should not give people **cause(= reason)** to worry. 연구원들은 자신들의 발견이 사람들에게 걱정의 원인이 되지 않을 것이라고 말한다. **대의** = purpose We hope you will support our organization's **cause(= purpose)** to educate young people. 젊은이들을 교육하고자 하는 저희 기관의 대의를 귀하가 지지해주시기를 바랍니다.
76 **challenge**	**문제** = problem They overcame the **challenge(= problem)** by working together to find a solution. 그들은 해결책을 찾기 위해 함께 일하여 문제를 극복해냈다.
77 **coalition**	**연합** = alliance The two political parties joined together to form a powerful **coalition(= alliance)**. 두 정당은 강력한 연합을 만들기 위해 힘을 합쳤다.
78 **commission**	**보수** = payment For every sale, they receive a **commission(= payment)** of 5 percent of the total selling price. 모든 매출에서, 그들은 전체 판매가의 5퍼센트의 보수를 받는다.
79 **conclusion**	**결과** = result The research team discussed the **conclusions(= results)** from their study in the report. 연구팀은 보고서에서 그들의 연구로부터 나온 결과에 대해 논했다. **끝** = end These concerns were raised by the CEO at the **conclusion(= end)** of the meeting. 이러한 우려들은 회의의 끝 무렵 최고 경영자에 의해 제기되었다.
80 **contribution**	**헌신** = commitment As an accountant, I know to keep detailed records of donors' financial **contributions(= commitments)**. 회계 담당자로서, 저는 기부자들의 재정적 헌신에 대한 상세한 기록을 남겨야 함을 압니다.

81 **craft**	**기술 = skill** Learning a new **craft(= skill)** is a good way to keep occupied during retirement. 새로운 기술을 배우는 것은 은퇴 생활 동안 바쁘게 지내는 좋은 방법이다. **배 = ship** The **craft(= ship)** hit a rock as it approached land and started to sink into the water. 배는 육지로 다가가다가 바위에 부딪쳤고 물속으로 가라앉기 시작했다.
82 **deficiency**	**부족 = shortage** The town was abandoned when a long absence of rain led to a severe **deficiency(= shortage)** of water. 마을은 오랜 가뭄이 심각한 물 부족을 야기했을 때 버려졌다.
83 **demand**	**수요 = desire** New businesses are usually launched in response to an unfulfilled customer **demand(= desire)**. 신규 사업은 보통 만족되지 못한 고객 수요에 대한 반응으로 시작된다.
84 **drawback**	**결점 = weakness** The main **drawback(= weakness)** of the product was that it only worked when there was enough sunlight. 그 제품의 주된 결점은 그것이 충분한 햇빛이 있을 때만 작동한다는 것이었다. **난점 = difficulty** The **drawback(= difficulty)** was that the inventors had to face the plastic industry in order to reduce packaging wastes. 난점은 개발자들이 포장 폐기물을 줄이기 위해 플라스틱 업계에 맞서야 한다는 것이었다.
85 **expansion**	**확장 = extension** Investment is needed to fund the **expansion(= extension)** of our services to overseas markets. 저희 서비스의 해외 시장으로의 확장에 자금을 대기 위해 투자가 필요합니다.
86 **feature**	**특징 = characteristic** The building's **features(= characteristics)** are typical of ancient Greek architecture. 그 건물의 특징은 고대 그리스 건축 양식을 대표한다.
87 **fruition**	**성과 = completion** We expect the project to come to **fruition(= completion)** by the end of the year. 저희는 이 프로젝트가 올해 말쯤에는 성과가 있을 것이라고 예상합니다.
88 **inclination**	**좋아함 = liking** She showed an **inclination(= liking)** for acting from a very young age. 그녀는 아주 어릴 때부터 연기를 좋아함을 보여주었다.

89 indication	현상 = effect
	Additional testing produced some **indication(= effect)** to suggest that the initial findings were false.
	추가 실험은 초기 발견이 사실이 아니었음을 암시하는 몇 가지 현상을 보여주었다.

90 mark	상징 = symbol
	Many consumers now recognize our logo as a **mark(= symbol)** of quality.
	많은 소비자들은 이제 저희 로고를 우수함의 상징으로 여깁니다.
	점수 = score
	Less than half the participants received a high **mark(= score)** on the test.
	절반이 안 되는 참가자들이 시험에서 높은 점수를 받았다.
	목표 = target
	We fell a little bit short of our **mark(= target)** of attracting 100,000 people to the job fair.
	저희는 취업 박람회에 10만 명을 끌어모으고자 했던 목표에 아주 조금 못 미쳤습니다.

91 objective	목적 = goal
	The study's main **objective(= goal)** is to learn how coral reefs respond to heat.
	연구의 주목적은 산호초가 열에 어떻게 반응하는지를 알아내는 것이다.

92 particular	세부 사항 = detail
	A report will be issued discussing the **particulars(= details)** of the meeting.
	회의에서 다뤄진 세부 사항들을 논하는 보고서가 발행될 것입니다.

93 patron	후원자 = supporter
	Lorenzo de' Medici used his wealth to become a well-known **patron (= supporter)** of the arts.
	로렌초 데 메디치는 예술의 유명한 후원자가 되기 위해 그의 재산을 사용했다.
	고객 = customer
	Over a million loyal **patrons(= customers)** visited our stores last year.
	백만 명이 넘는 단골 고객들이 작년에 저희 가게를 방문해주셨습니다.

94 phase	단계 = stage
	The insect undergoes physical changes at various **phases(= stages)** in its development.
	곤충은 발달하는 과정의 여러 단계에서 물리적인 변화를 겪는다.

95 priority	우선 = preference
	Our **priority(= preference)** would be to finish work on the current project before starting a new one.
	우리는 새 프로젝트를 시작하기 전에 현재의 프로젝트를 끝내는 것이 우선일 것이다.

96 **proximity**	**접근성** = nearness The center's **proximity(= nearness)** to various attractions makes it an ideal place to hold your event. 센터의 다양한 명소와의 접근성은 귀사의 행사를 개최하기에 이상적인 장소로 만듭니다.
97 **reward**	**보답** = return The company offers cash to users in **reward(= return)** for reporting bugs in its software. 그 회사는 소프트웨어상의 오류를 신고하는 사용자에게 보답으로 현금을 제공한다.
98 **riddle**	**수수께끼** = puzzle Sending a probe to the planet will help scientists answer the **riddle(= puzzle)** of how it formed. 행성에 탐사선을 보내는 것은 과학자들이 그 행성이 어떻게 형성되었는지에 대한 수수께끼를 푸는 데 도움이 될 것이다.
99 **scope**	**범위** = range Including thousands of participants, the multi-year study is impressive in its **scope(= range)**. 수천 명의 참가자를 포함해서, 다년간의 연구는 그 범위가 인상적이다.
100 **sensation**	**선풍을 일으키는 것** = hit The movie was a **sensation(= hit)**, dominating conversation everywhere. 그 영화는 모든 곳에서 가장 중요한 이야깃거리가 되는, 선풍을 일으키는 것이었다. **감각** = feeling Touching a hot stove creates a painful **sensation(= feeling)**. 뜨거운 난로를 만지는 것은 고통스러운 감각을 불러일으킨다.
101 **settlement**	**정착지** = community Human **settlements(= communities)** throughout history have tended to form near bodies of water. 역사 전반에 걸친 인류의 정착지는 물줄기 가까이에 형성되는 경향이 있었다. **식민지** = colony The **settlements(= colonies)** established by the Phoenicians were used as trading posts. 페니키아인들이 세운 식민지는 교역소로 사용되었다.
102 **solidarity**	**연대** = unity Protests were held in many cities to show **solidarity(= unity)** with the laborers on strike. 파업 중인 노동자들과의 연대를 보여주기 위해 많은 도시에서 시위가 열렸다.
103 **subject**	**대상** = individual The study recruited over 2,000 **subjects(= individuals)** ranging in age from 55 to 64. 연구는 55세에서 64세 사이의 2천 명이 넘는 대상들을 모집했다.

104 **system**	**체제** = structure
	The country was forced to change its **system(= structure)** of government.
	국가는 정부 체제를 바꿀 수밖에 없었다.

105 **testament**	**증거** = proof
	Her long career is a **testament(= proof)** to her abilities as a performer.
	그녀의 오랜 경력은 연기자로서 그녀의 능력에 대한 증거이다.

3. 형용사

106 **acute**	**예리한** = sharp
	Their **acute(= sharp)** sense of hearing helps foxes to hunt for prey at night.
	여우의 예리한 청력은 그들이 밤에 먹이 사냥을 할 수 있게 도와준다.
	중대한 = crucial
	The government faced an **acute(= crucial)** emergency as homes across the region lost power.
	정부는 그 지역의 집들이 전력을 공급받지 못해 중대한 비상사태에 직면했다.

107 **adverse**	**해로운** = harmful
	Eating too much sugar produces **adverse(= harmful)** effects in the human body.
	설탕을 너무 많이 먹는 것은 인체에 해로운 결과를 낳는다.

108 **apprehensive**	**우려하는** = worried
	Some of the employees are **apprehensive(= worried)** about losing their jobs if the company fails.
	몇몇 직원들은 회사가 파산하여 그들이 직업을 잃게 되는 것을 우려한다.

109 **bold**	**대담한** = daring
	Carson's **bold(= daring)** ideas in *Silent Spring* gave birth to the modern ecological movement.
	「침묵의 봄」에서 카슨의 대담한 사상은 근대 생태 운동을 탄생시켰다.

110 **close**	**가까운** = near
	We moved our office so that we could be **close(= near)** to our clients.
	저희는 고객과 더 가까울 수 있도록 사무실을 옮겼습니다.
	친한 = friendly
	The two gradually grew **close(= friendly)** after meeting on a film set.
	영화 세트장에서 만난 후 그 둘은 점차 친해졌다.

111 **considerable**	**많은** = large The project will require a **considerable(= large)** investment of time and money to succeed. 프로젝트는 성공하기 위해 많은 시간과 돈의 투자를 필요로 할 것이다.
112 **deep**	**심오한** = meaningful The novel provides **deep(= meaningful)** insight into the experience of women in the Victorian era. 그 소설은 빅토리아 시대 여성들의 경험에 대한 심오한 통찰을 제공한다.
113 **eerie**	**무서운** = scary The director is renowned for the **eerie(= scary)** atmosphere of his films, which are often set in creepy old houses. 그 감독은 종종 으스스한 옛집을 배경으로 하는 그의 영화들의 무서운 분위기로 유명하다.
114 **elementary**	**기초적인** = undeveloped She persisted despite having only an **elementary(= undeveloped)** understanding of the industry. 그녀는 그 산업에 대한 기초적인 이해밖에 없었음에도 일을 계속했다.
115 **endemic**	**특유의** = exclusive Because of the island's remoteness, it has many **endemic(= exclusive)** plants and animals. 섬의 고립성 때문에, 그곳에는 특유의 많은 식물과 동물이 있다.
116 **fragile**	**취약한** = delicate Some ecosystems are extremely **fragile(= delicate)** and sensitive to any small changes. 어떤 생태계는 극히 취약하여 작은 변화에도 민감하다.
117 **impolite**	**무례한** = rude It is considered **impolite(= rude)** to interrupt other people who are speaking during a meeting. 회의 중에 말하고 있는 다른 사람에게 끼어드는 것은 무례하다고 여겨진다.
118 **instantaneous**	**즉각적인** = immediate Certain chemicals produced an **instantaneous(= immediate)** reaction when mixed together. 특정 화학 물질들은 섞이면서 즉각적인 반응을 보였다.
119 **intricate**	**복잡한** = complex Trade agreements are governed by **intricate(= complex)** rules which all parties must follow. 무역 협정은 모든 당사자들이 따라야 하는 복잡한 규칙에 의해 지배된다.

120 **malicious**	**악의적인** = immoral Religious authorities attacked anyone they felt was engaged in **malicious (= immoral)** acts. 종교 당국은 악의적인 행위에 가담했다고 생각된 사람은 누구든 공격했다.
121 **momentous**	**중대한** = important His **momentous(= important)** decision altered the course of his nation's history. 그의 중대한 결정은 국가의 역사 전개를 바꿔 놓았다.
122 **natural**	**천연의** = pure Our product contains only **natural(= pure)** ingredients and no added chemicals. 저희 제품은 화학 첨가물 없이 천연 재료만 포함합니다. **타고난** = native As a football player, he displayed tremendous **natural(= native)** ability at a very young age. 축구 선수로서, 그는 아주 어린 나이에 대단한 타고난 재능을 보였다.
123 **negligible**	**사소한** = unimportant The suggested changes were minor and had only a **negligible (= unimportant)** impact on our business. 제안된 변경 사항은 대수롭지 않아 저희 사업에는 사소한 영향만 끼쳤습니다.
124 **original**	**최초의** = earliest In its **original(= earliest)** sense, the word "nice" used to mean "stupid" or "ignorant." 최초의 의미로는, "nice"라는 단어는 "어리석은"이나 "무지한"을 의미하곤 했다.
125 **pending**	**완료되지 않은** = unfinished He had a lot of **pending(= unfinished)** tasks that were due to be finished soon so he declined their invitation to dinner. 그는 곧 끝내야 할 완료되지 않은 업무가 많아 그들의 저녁 식사 초대를 거절했다.
126 **perilous**	**위험한** = risky The explorers endured a **perilous(= risky)** journey across the steep mountain path. 탐험가들은 가파른 산길을 지나는 위험한 여정을 견뎌냈다.
127 **positive**	**좋은** = good She earned **positive(= good)** feedback for her performance from critics and audiences alike. 그녀는 비평가들과 관중들 모두로부터 그녀의 연기에 대한 좋은 피드백을 받았다.
128 **previous**	**이전의** = earlier Our latest product is far more advanced than **previous(= earlier)** models. 저희의 최신 제품은 이전 모델보다 훨씬 더 발전했습니다.

129 **reasonable**	**적당한** = moderate
	The hockey team thought that they had a **reasonable(= moderate)** chance of winning the match. 하키팀은 그들이 시합을 이길 적당한 가능성이 있다고 생각했다.

130 **rival**	**경쟁하는** = competing
	Coca Cola's market share grew to become roughly twice that of its nearest **rival(= competing)** company, Pepsi. 코카콜라의 시장 점유율은 그들의 가장 가까운 경쟁사인 펩시의 약 두 배가 될 만큼 커졌다.

131 **scarce**	**부족한** = limited
	Having **scarce(= limited)** resources of its own, the country attacked neighboring states. 국가 자체적으로 부족한 자원을 갖고 있었기 때문에, 그 국가는 이웃 국가들을 공격했다.

132 **severe**	**심각한** = serious
	Having to pay the new trade tariff has had a **severe(= serious)** effect on our profits, which are now much lower. 새로운 무역 관세를 지불해야 하는 것은 우리의 수익에 심각한 영향을 미쳤고, 수익은 현재 훨씬 적다.

133 **skeptical**	**회의적인** = doubtful
	Producers were **skeptical(= doubtful)** at first that the actor could play the role. 제작자는 그 배우가 그 역할을 할 수 있을 것이라는 데에 처음에는 회의적이었다.

134 **sophisticated**	**세련된** = stylish
	Audrey Hepburn was equally known for her **sophisticated(= stylish)** sense of fashion. 오드리 헵번은 그녀의 세련된 패션 감각으로도 알려졌다.
	복잡한 = complex
	The manufacturing process makes use of **sophisticated(= complex)** robotic equipment. 그 제조 과정은 복잡한 로봇 장비를 사용한다.

135 **staple**	**기본적인** = basic
	Milk is a **staple(= basic)** product that should be available to everyone at a low price. 우유는 모든 사람이 저렴한 비용으로 구할 수 있어야 하는 기본적인 제품이다.

136 **subsequent**	**결과로 초래되는** = resulting
	The study discusses work stressors and their **subsequent(= resulting)** effect on employee morale. 연구는 업무 스트레스 요인과 그것의 결과로 초래되는 직원들의 사기에 미치는 영향에 대해 논한다.

137 **succeeding**	**다음의** = following
	Product sales were strong at first, but declined over the **succeeding (= following)** months. 제품 매출은 처음에는 견고했으나, 다음 몇 개월 동안 하락했다.

138 vulnerable	**취약한** = helpless
	The genetic disease makes sufferers **vulnerable(= helpless)** if they contract any form of virus.
	유전병은 만약 환자들이 어떤 형태의 바이러스에 걸리면 그것에 취약하게 만든다.

4. 부사

139 aptly	**알맞게** = fittingly
	The spaceflight program was **aptly(= fittingly)** named after Mercury, the Roman god of travelers.
	우주 비행 프로그램은 여행자의 로마 신 머큐리의 이름을 따서 알맞게 명명되었다.

140 credibly	**정확하게** = faithfully
	The Edwardian period is portrayed **credibly(= faithfully)** in the movie, with great attention to detail.
	세세한 부분까지 주목하여, 에드워디언 시대가 그 영화에 정확하게 묘사되어 있다.

141 discreetly	**신중히** = carefully
	He **discreetly(= carefully)** checked his appearance in the mirror before leaving the office.
	그는 사무실을 떠나기 전에 거울 속 자신의 모습을 신중히 살폈다.

142 exclusively	**독점적으로** = solely
	The investment firm caters **exclusively(= solely)** to individuals with extensive assets.
	그 투자 회사는 막대한 자산을 가진 개인에게 독점적으로 서비스를 제공한다.

143 instinctively	**무의식적으로** = automatically
	As the CEO walked past the desks, employees **instinctively(= automatically)** sat up a little straighter.
	최고 경영자가 책상을 지나쳐 걸어갔을 때, 직원들은 무의식적으로 조금 더 똑바로 앉았다.

144 intently	**진지하게** = seriously
	We listened **intently(= seriously)** to the concerns you raised and have introduced some changes.
	저희는 귀하가 언급한 염려를 진지하게 들었으며 몇 가지 변경을 도입했습니다.

145 sparingly	**드물게** = infrequently
	The drug must be used **sparingly(= infrequently)** to prevent patients from developing addictions.
	약은 환자가 중독되는 것을 방지하기 위해 드물게 사용되어야 한다.

MEMO

G-TELP KOREA 공식 지정

2주 만에 끝내는

해커스 지텔프 독해 LEVEL 2

개정 2판 7쇄 발행 2024년 9월 2일
개정 2판 1쇄 발행 2021년 8월 30일

지은이	해커스 어학연구소
펴낸곳	㈜해커스 어학연구소
펴낸이	해커스 어학연구소 출판팀
주소	서울특별시 서초구 강남대로61길 23 ㈜해커스 어학연구소
고객센터	02-537-5000
교재 관련 문의	publishing@hackers.com
동영상강의	HackersIngang.com
ISBN	978-89-6542-434-5 (13740)
Serial Number	02-07-01

외국어인강 1위,
해커스인강 HackersIngang.com

해커스인강

• 전문 스타강사의 **G-TELP 공식 기출문제 동영상강의**
• 들으면서 외우는 **G-TELP 필수 단어암기장 및 단어암기 MP3**

영어 전문 포털,
해커스영어 Hackers.co.kr

해커스영어

• 무료 **G-TELP 단기 고득점 비법 강의**
• 무료 지텔프/공무원/세무사/회계사 **시험정보 및 학습자료**

헤럴드 선정 2018 대학생 선호브랜드 대상 '대학생이 선정한 외국어인강' 부문 1위